Turning Small Talk

into

Big Talk

THE POWER
OF A
QUESTION

Turning
Small Talk
into
Big Talk

JAN JANURA

Forefront
BOOKS

Turning Small Talk into Big Talk: The Power of a Question

Copyright © 2022 by Jan Janura

Library of Congress Control Number: 2022912014

Print ISBN: 978-1-63763-119-5
E-book ISBN: 978-1-63763-120-1

Published in Association with Yates & Yates, www.Yates2.com

Cover Design by Bruce Gore, Gore Studio, Inc.
Interior Design by Bill Kersey, KerseyGraphics

This book is dedicated to
Conrad Jacobsen, my Young Life club leader in
Hinsdale, Illinois, who patiently helped me make the
most important decision of my life.

and

Don Reeverts, my lifelong mentor.

and

Doug Coe, the most interesting person I ever met!

Foreword

by Hugh Hewitt

When Jan Janura took a seat on my patio in Southern California in the early summer of 2009 and lit up a cigar, I'd already heard of him, often, from our mutual friend, Bud. Jan was a fabulously successful businessman who had begun his adult life with an advanced degree from Fuller Theological Seminary, at the same time as had Bud, and had taken a job as a Young Life Area Director in the Seattle area. (Bud had done the same thing in Orange County, California.) Jan picked up fly fishing during that first stint in ministry, as well as the self-awareness that he was called to business.

Was he ever. Along with his wife, Carol Anderson, Jan founded, built, and sold not one but two very successful businesses. At the age most folks retire and look to ease back and enjoy life, he embarked on a different kind of mission.

This time, Jan would initially focus on men over the age of 40, the "up and outers," who were looking to figure out where they were in their lives, their relationships with God and their spouses and families, and where the "second half" or "third third" would take them. That focus required getting to know people, often in the unusually constrained hours of a long lunch or a leisurely dinner.

When Jan tracked me down, it was because Carol had heard one of my closest friends, Bill Lobdell, talking on my radio show about his then new book *Losing My Religion*. At that time, Bill was the reporter for religion for the Los Angeles Times, and his crisis of faith is detailed in his book. Carol concluded that Bill needed to join Jan on one of his Wild Adventures in Montana, so Jan sought me out to seek out Bill.

The happy by-product of Jan's mission to my backyard is a deep friendship over that has lasted over 14 years, at least as many time zones, and a thousand emails, calls, and conversations. Some people collect wine —including Jan— and some fly fish with a passion and excellence that few sports inspire in any but the youngest athletes. That's Jan too. But his hobbies have always been in service of his mission. Through these 14 years, Jan's theme has been to make time count, never to waste it, to refuse to slow down, and to do as much as he can for as many as he can for as long as he can.

Jan's mission to men has been multi-faceted. He and Carol are, objectively, two of those most generous people on the planet towards those for whom life has been hard. They are also both terrific encouragers to those for whom life has been an adventure and a success in the eyes of the world. But Jan is defined by his mission to get men to ask the most serious questions, questions almost everyone asks themselves but rarely pose to each other or to a group.

Jan's been organizing small fishing trips for men for more than twice as long as I've known him. He institutionalized "The Wild Adventure" early in the new century to broaden and deepen the reach of his ministry. He expanded his chronological reach by starting the "Young Guns" portion of TWA.us. He has packed friends on to boats and into meeting rooms in wonderful locations with the only objective being that they engage in some serious conversations about serious subjects.

Now Jan has put into this compelling, winsome, and wise book the weight-bearing wall of his approach: Ask the right questions and people will actually talk about everything that is on their hearts and in their heads. But it starts with the right questions. Perhaps one the question above all others being, "Who do you say I am?"

Jan's ministry is about as far from "church" as you can go. It has little-to-nothing in common with "men's ministry" and "Bible study groups."

If you have heard Jan on my radio show —he's been a frequent guest for the past decade— you will know his infectious and deep-throated laugh. "A constant cheerfulness is the surest sign of wisdom" the French essayist Montaigne penned hundreds of years ago. Jan and Michel would have been the closest of friends, and not just because of their endless good cheer or their addiction to well-turned phrases and memorable quotations. (Montaigne covered the ceiling of his study with his favorite quotes. Jan reduces them to beautiful index cards and sends them off to his legions of friends.)

They would be bound by their seriousness of purpose hidden within an east amiability, a love of good things, a wonderful family and many friends, and most of all, a desire to know the most important things, a desire best met not with answers, but the right questions.

-Hugh Hewitt

Table of Contents

The Problem
with
Small Talk

Can you remember the last time you had a significant conversation with your wife or husband, your kids, your best friend, or anybody? When was the last time you walked across your lawn and sat on a neighbor's front porch and talked with him or her—and truly listened—over a cup of coffee or iced tea?

I'm not talking about the conversations we have on social media nowadays, whether it's through one hundred and forty characters or less on Twitter or on Facebook Messenger. I'm talking about real face-to-face conversations, in which you're truly listening to what someone else is saying, and you're talking deeply about the subjects that matter most in life. I'm not referring to small talk, which each of us can easily do with our thumbs and our phones or in face-to-face conversations that are dull and never scratch the surface.

I'm talking about Big Talk, in which we dig deep into our souls and discuss intriguing topics that shape our world and impact our daily lives. Conversation is undoubtedly the most important part of a relationship, whether it's business, personal, or spiritual. It's the only way to truly get to know someone, and it's the best method for strengthening your bond with your spouse, your children, friends, business associates, and even God.

Each of us wants to interact with others, and all of us long to be heard. Conversation is almost as important as water and oxygen when it comes to living a truly fulfilling life. The conversations each one of us chooses to have can change the world—or destroy it—and the words, questions, and answers each of us choose to use, or not to use, can alter our own life and the lives of everyone around us. So, why wouldn't we choose to make our conversations as impactful and important as we can?

> I'm talking about Big Talk, in which we dig deep into our souls and discuss intriguing topics that shape our world and impact our daily lives.

Before we go any further, let me take a moment to introduce myself. My name is Jan Janura, and I spent more than forty years in the women's fashion business alongside my partner, Carol Anderson—she was the fashion, and I was the business. And oh, by the way, after more than sixteen years as business associates, Carol and I realized we were in love and became true partners as husband and wife!

In case you're wondering, this isn't a book about the apparel business. Thank goodness! This is a book about how to lead significant conversations that will change your life. But in many ways, much of what I've learned about turning small talk into Big Talk began with addressing a major need in my business. So, I'll take a little time to share that story.

Carol and I became friends back in the early seventies while I was attending Fuller Theological Seminary in Pasadena, California. After graduation, I moved to Seattle and worked as an area director for Young Life, a nonprofit Christian organization that focuses on ministering to young people in middle school, high school, and college. Working for Young Life was one of the most rewarding experiences of my life, but after four years, I felt a calling to start a business.

At twenty-seven years old, I interviewed for a position at IBM. The job I was applying for would have allowed me to learn about business and continue my education. And the good news was, IBM was going to pay me to do this. I went through two days of interviews and felt good about landing the job. Someone from IBM called me three days later and said, "Jan, it was great to meet you, but you're not quite what we're looking for." I was devastated. I thought I'd totally misread what God was saying to me. I was worried that I'd left a fantastic position with Young Life and four of the most substantive years of my life for nothing. It was really a low point for me.

By that time, Carol had become a successful fashion designer, and we had remained friends, exchanging birthday and Christmas cards. I had recently traveled to Washington, D.C., where I heard the most interesting man I've ever met in my life, Doug Coe, speak about covenant relationships, a partnership in which two parties make binding promises to each other and work together to reach a common goal. Immediately, Carol was the person who came to mind. We had volunteered together in Young Life while I was attending seminary. We shared many of the same beliefs and goals in life. As soon as I left that event in Washington, D.C., I found a phone and called her.

Carol was happy I had reached out because she, too, was struggling to make some important decisions about her career and future. She had just left a company where she had been working for nine years. She was entertaining offers from four or five other outfits but was also seriously considering going out on her own. Immediately, I knew the timing was right for us to become partners. I guess it was God tugging at my heart.

"Let's start a company," I told her.

Her response: "You're insane. You don't know anything about the apparel industry."

I asked Carol to think about it for a couple of weeks and get back to me. Fortunately for both of us, she came around to my crazy idea. It ended up being a life-changing moment for both of us—in more ways than one. Carol was taking a leap of faith because I hadn't worked in the clothing industry before and had never owned a business. Yet, I knew it was God's plan for me. In my heart, I knew how talented Carol was. She had a gift. I believed it was my job to build an infrastructure around her so that she could freely work her magic.

In 1977, we started Carol Anderson, INC., on an eight hundred-dollar investment in the garage of a home in Burbank, California. Carol's father came out from Omaha, Nebraska, to build shelves in the garage. Carol had a sewing machine and went to work. We started with twelve garments, and I managed to get us an appointment with a Nordstrom buyer in Seattle. The buyer agreed to give us a test order to see if Carol's clothes would sell.

Not long after that, we moved into a ninth-floor loft in the garment district of Los Angeles. We had nothing—and I mean nothing—to put in the space. The day after we signed the lease, two buyers from Nordstrom delivered a $35,000 order. We were off and running. After Carol designed the garments, we had them manufactured and anxiously waited for a response. The results were good: Carol's clothes were selling and Nordstrom wanted more.

Over the next twenty-five years, we built Carol Anderson, INC., into one of the most recognized and successful lines of women's dress and casual sports-wear in the world. Our business grew to $35 million annually—despite the fact we didn't have a single storefront. Our clothes were being sold in stores such as Nordstrom and Neiman Marcus and were being exported to Austria, Germany, Switzerland, and other countries around the world. We had twenty-four sales-people on the road and were selling to three thousand retail outlets and high-end boutiques. Vanna White wore our clothes on *Wheel of Fortune*, and they were given away as prizes on other shows like *The Price Is Right*.

By then, however, I was beginning to realize that the clothing business was changing rapidly. Most of the major department stores were consolidating, which meant the remaining buyers began to have a huge amount of leverage. In fact, rather than us presenting Carol's designs and taking orders at our prices, the remaining retailers started telling us how much they were willing to pay for each item. They were even asking us to buy back what we didn't sell, which was squeezing our profit margins. In short, the golden age of domestic apparel manufacturing was coming to an end.

To stay in the game, I knew I had to find a way to get Carol's wonderful creations into the hands of customers without relying on our retail partners any longer. But how was I going to do that? After a brief experiment with catalogs, I was having break-fast one morning and sketched out the concept on the proverbial napkin at breakfast on how we might take Carol's creations direct to the consumer. I had always been fascinated with the way Tupperware did that, and I thought the same general concept might be able to work. Actually, based on my cash-flow projections, I felt like this new idea could be a game changer and possibly an industry disruptor—if we could figure out how to execute it.

My idea was to set up a distribution model where we would contract with women to sell our apparel directly to their friends and neighbors in their homes, skipping the retail stores altogether. It was kind of like Tupperware for women's clothing. No one had ever attempted it before in the way I had envisioned it.

By the way, you may have heard of the result: it's a company called CAbi (an acronym for Carol Anderson by Invitation), which is still in operation today. Carol and I started the business in 2003 and sold it ten years later, when we had more than 3,400 associates (or stylists) working to sell our products—which made us the largest direct-sales company in the world for our industry. It was truly a wild ride!

Of course, back in the very beginning, I knew that in order for my model to work, I needed to find the right people to help sell and distribute my wife's wonderful designs. But which people were the right people?

• • •

To answer that question, Carol and I started hosting dinner parties of eight to twelve people each. We did this once, twice, or sometimes even three times a week—inviting people we knew, and then encouraging them to invite their friends, and then their friends' friends, and so on. We thought this might be a great way to expand our contacts and build up a network of potential salespeople.

My secret goal was to keep watch each evening and see which women emerged as the leaders within the group. I wanted to see who carried the interest and attention of the other guests—who had the most attractive personalities. Who were the women who communicated well, listened even better, were humble, could motivate others to succeed, and had the ability to connect people with a purpose? Those were the women we would recruit to join us at CAbi.

Doesn't that sound like a good business idea? It certainly did to me. But very early on, it became apparent that our dinners were not turning out to be the lively social events Carol and I had envisioned. As soon as the first few guests arrived, little pockets of conversation would spring up around the table. Most of them were quiet pockets, with people talking softly in groups of two or three, sometimes even huddling close together rather than looking outward to include others. Whoops! Worst of all, every conversation was on a different topic, and each one stayed on the surface, never daring to go below to find out what others thought or felt about things that truly mattered.

Obviously, it was beyond difficult to figure out which women were leaders when all I could observe were these little huddles of subdued and superficial chitchat. In fact, it was downright impossible, which is one of the reasons I seriously began to hate small talk in all its forms. What a waste of our precious time!

Around this same time, the woman sitting next to me at the dinner table spoke up.

"Hello, Jan. So good to see you again," she said, while smoothing her dress and patting her hair to make sure it had stayed in place.

I recognized her face, but I couldn't remember her name. Yikes! *Is it Jennifer?* I asked myself. *Maybe Jessica?*

"I'm Julie," she said.

"Hi, Julie. Thanks for coming," I replied.

Whew! I thought. Thank goodness, and good thing I had kept my mouth shut.

Only a few of our dinner guests had arrived at that point, so Julie and I were alone at one corner of the table. Carol was already in conversation with another woman across from me, four seats away. I was too far away to hear much of what they were saying.

Julie looked around the room for a minute, then turned back to me without saying a word. The silence stretched toward the point of awkwardness.

"Got any kids?" I asked.

Julie's eyes brightened immediately. "Oh yes," she said, patting her purse. "I'm a proud soccer mom, and I've got the minivan to prove it!"

That's when I made a mistake. If I'd known what was about to happen, I would have filled my mouth with some of the excellent wine on the table—or even gravel for that matter—and I would have kept it that way until the final course!

Instead, I asked, "Do any of your kids actually play soccer?"

"Of course!" Julie exclaimed exuberantly. It was almost as if she'd been waiting for me to ask that exact question.

"My Elizabeth—she's the oldest—she just made the varsity team this year and she's only a sophomore! Did you know that sophomores could be recruited up to the varsity team?"

I started to shake my head, but Julie was already moving forward.

"I was so surprised when Elizabeth told me the coaches had chosen her, although I wasn't really surprised, because she's always been advanced for her age—really, anytime she puts her mind to anything, she just makes it happen, and that's exactly how it was with soccer ever since she was a little girl because she scored a goal in the very first game she ever played. No, actually it was two goals! She was only seven back then, but she..."

Over the next two hours, I discovered that Julie was indeed a soccer mom—a very talkative soccer mom. A very talkative soccer mom who never seemed to get tired of telling me all about her daughter, who I'm sure was a lovely young girl, and did I mention that she was a fantastic soccer player?

Needless to say, I had a frustrating dining experience served up to me all through that very long evening!

• • •

How many times have you been in a similar situation? The art of engaging with others in a way that is thoughtful and interesting has been largely lost in today's world. As a result, deep and meaningful conversations are almost impossible to find—especially in social settings. Guys don't always want to talk about sports or the weather, and ladies don't always want to talk about the latest shoes or the new hunk on *The Bachelor*.

Unfortunately, most conversations today are transactional. They serve as a means to an end—as a way of requesting and dispensing information. "Where did you find this coffee?" "Do you have plans for dinner on Friday night?" "What time does the game start?"

When we do actually take the time for larger and longer conversations—during a dinner party, for example, or gathered in a living room or around a campfire—what we say almost always stays at the surface. We talk about the weather, sports, fashion, or the latest celebrity gossip. In other words, we settle for small talk—for chitchat.

Now, there's nothing wrong with small talk in and of itself. But there's not much right about it, either! Ultimately, small talk and chitchat are simply ways of passing time without seeming rude during social situations. They have no significance. And I've reached a point in my life where I'm tired of wasting my time, treasure, and talent on things that are insignificant.

I believe the absence of serious, meaningful conversations is the root of many of the problems in our society today. We can't talk about serious subjects like politics, our hopes and fears, problems in our cities, religion, our regrets, and stress and health problems that might be tearing us down. More times than not, these conversations turn into shouting matches or uncomfortable moments because we've been trained to avoid those subjects at all costs. Or, even worse, the person we're trying to engage throws up walls of protection and becomes silent or quickly changes the subject. We no longer know how to discuss heavy topics, even with our spouses, partners, children, and closest friends. It shouldn't be that way, and it's not healthy.

> You don't have to be content with shallow interactions, whether at the dinner table or anyplace else. You don't have to waste your time with small talk. You can go deeper and help others do the same.

If you feel the same way, I've got good news: you don't have to settle for chitchat! This little book you're holding will teach you the large and useful skill of turning small talk into Big Talk through the power of table questions. You're probably asking yourself, *What are table questions?* They are thoughtful, intentional questions designed to help people move below the surface and experience deep, meaningful conversations—the kinds of conversations that are not only interesting, but are sometimes even life-changing.

We'll learn more about what table questions are and how to use them through the rest of this book.

But for now, I want to emphasize again that you don't have to be content with shallow interactions, whether at the dinner table or anyplace else. You don't have to waste your time with small talk. You can go deeper and help others do the same, and I'm excited to show you how!

• • •

Carol and I did our best to spice up each dinner party as we searched for the women who would help us build our new company. We tried to be more engaging and enthusiastic ourselves. We tried to position ourselves at strategic points around the table. But it felt like we were blocked at every turn. Each of us could only engage with one or two people at each dinner, and we weren't getting to know anyone on a deeper level.

Julie was the final straw—my soccer mom extraordinaire. By the time she finally released me after that long, long evening, I knew we had to come up with a different plan for our dinners. But what could we do? I was feeling desperate and disillusioned, and we were running out of time.

Thankfully, the answer struck me just a few days later. It was so simple, yet also so profound. I knew right away it was genius!

PART I

Setting
the
Table

I'm a resident of Montana, which means I get to spend six or seven months out of every year in one of the most beautiful places on the planet. Montana is often referred to as "Big Sky Country," and that's certainly true. But it's what you can find beneath that sky that I like best.

If you're like millions of other Americans, you have probably seen Montana's beauty on the hit TV show *Yellowstone*, in which the actor Kevin Costner plays rancher John Dutton. There's a reason Dutton and his family fight so hard to keep their ranch out of the hands of developers and rivals. There is no other place in the world like Montana. It's why the novelist John Steinbeck once wrote that he was in love with the state.

Our home is nestled into a glacier-carved valley at the feet of the Madison Range of the Rocky Mountains, which is a group of mountains that rises more than ten thousand feet above sea level, which we look at. In the early nineteenth century, Lewis and Clark named the range in honor of future U.S. President James Madison, who was then the U.S. secretary of state. The Native Americans used to refer to the Madison Range as the "Shining Mountains" because of the way they both capture and reflect the light of the sun. I especially love how the snow-topped rock faces can change from bright earth tones in the full light of the afternoon to muted blues and purples as the sun sets each evening.

I also live next to the Madison River, which has been recognized for decades as one of the best fly-fishing rivers in the world. The Madison begins in Yellowstone National Park and flows for more than one hundred and forty miles through some of the most picturesque scenery God has created. Near the town of Three Forks, Montana, it joins with the Gallatin and Jefferson Rivers to form the Missouri River. Floating the Madison is an incredible experience. Not only is the scenery amazing and the fishing world class, but you're joined by bald eagles, osprey, red-tailed hawks, and other raptors as you glide around bends and slip between boulders.

Thirty-six years ago, in Seattle, I discovered my love for fly-fishing. I was twenty-four years old and single, and I needed a hobby. I went to the only Eddie Bauer store in Seattle —back then it was the first such store before it became a nationwide chain—and purchased a fly rod reel and line for thirty-nine dollars. While I was waiting in line to pay, a guy named Earl Love asked me, "Son, have you ever cast a fly rod before?"

"No," I told him.

Earl took me up to the sixth-floor roof, put my rod and reel together, and showed me how to cast. Before I could go fly-fishing, Earl told me, I had to practice in the backyard for thirty minutes every night for a month. By the end of the month, I was ready to go fly-fishing. It was the most fun thing I had ever done. I had played football in high school and rock climbed and skied competitively when I went to college in Colorado, but I discovered there was nothing more exhilarating than fly-fishing.

What I loved most about fly-fishing was that to do it effectively, you had to forget about everything else. You had to focus on your tiny fly in the water and nothing else. Looking at your entire universe through a soda straw, it was easy to forget about whatever you might have been stressed out about that day. It was a wonderful time to relax. Eventually, I started taking my buddies up into the mountains to go fly-fishing. It was such a wonderful environment and so conducive to getting away from the noise in our lives.

There isn't a better river in the country than the Madison to catch wild rainbow trout and large brown trout. Trust me, there is no better feeling in the world than standing in a flowing river or brook with a fly rod in your hand, a cigar in your mouth, alone with only your thoughts and God, completely free of the congestion of the world.

Noted author Norman Maclean beautifully captured what the experience feels like in his acclaimed novel *A River Runs Through It*:

Like many fly fishermen in western Montana where the summer days are almost Arctic in length, I often do not start fishing until the cool of the evening. Then in the Arctic half-light of the canyon, all existence fades to a being with my soul and memories and the sounds of the Big Blackfoot River and a four-count rhythm and the hope that a fish will rise. Eventually, all things merge into one, and a river runs through it.[1]

Herbert Hoover, the thirty-first U.S. President who served from 1929 to 1933, might have described it even better when he wrote:

To go fishing is a sound, a valid, and an accepted reason for an escape. It requires no explanation. Nor is it the fish we get that counts. We could buy them in the market for mere silver at one percent of the cost. It is the chance to wash one's soul with pure air, with the rush of the brook, or with the shimmer of the sun on blue water. It brings meekness and inspiration from the decency of nature, charity toward tackle makers, patience toward fish, a mockery of profits and egos, a quieting of hate, a rejoicing that you do not have to decide a darned thing until next week. And it is discipline in the equality of men—for all men are equal before fish. And the contemplation of the water, the forest, and mountains soothes our troubles, shames our wickedness, and inspires us to esteem our fellowmen—especially other fishermen.[2]

This new hobby, my appreciation for the great outdoors and God's beauty, and my unmatched devotion to deep friendships all grew to become something more profound than I could have ever anticipated. It led me to combine my passion and hobby to create The Wild Adventure, a one-week excursion I host for groups of men at my Smiling Moose Ranch multiple times every summer. The Wild Adventure is about more than fly-fishing and camaraderie. It's also about having deep discussions about life's big questions. You'll learn more about that later in the book.

Yes, in my opinion, Montana truly is the "last best place." There is no place on earth as vast and beautiful as the western part of the United States. But it can also be a difficult and dangerous place—if you're not prepared.

Winter is especially treacherous. Those who choose to remain in Montana between November and May understand they need to be purposeful, not just to remain comfortable when the snow falls and the wind blows, but also to survive. Believe me, when the temperature drops to thirty below zero and the wind has piled ten-foot drifts of snow across the highways—that's a bad time to run out of supplies!

In a similar way, you need to be purposeful when it comes to transforming chitchat into serious dialogue. Just like preparing for a dinner party, it's vital that you prepare to move from the small talk that has been part of your life for so many years to a mindset of Big Talk.

To help you adjust your mindset, this book is divided into three parts. Part I focuses on setting the table by using table questions. You need to be intentional and willing to put some effort into preparing effectively. Part II focuses on fixing problem areas so you can be prepared to handle challenging scenarios that could arise. Part III focuses on putting the skills you have learned into practice by listening and considering sample questions.

> Just remember that you don't have to see the entire staircase to take the first step. Your journey might last one thousand miles, but every adventure requires a first step.

In life, I believe the most difficult thing to do is to take the first step. It's the hardest thing to do in starting a business. And it's the most challenging thing to do in starting a significant relationship. In both of those cases, it has risk and it's usually awkward because you've never done it before. There's a lot at stake. Just remember that you don't have to see the entire staircase to take the first step. Your journey might last one thousand miles, but every adventure requires a first step. The first time you use table questions, it may not work out perfectly, but I would almost guarantee that going for it—even if it feels awkward—will be better than not doing it at all. The second time will be smoother, and by the third attempt, you will have it nailed. A lot of people don't want to take that risk. That goes back to intentionality. Just remember that nothing great comes without risk. If you never take chances, you're not going to live a fulfilling life. Your life is going to be ordinary, and you will never reach your full potential.

In the early seventies, a young entrepreneur named Richard Smith dumped his life savings and millions of dollars in loans into a fledgling shipping company. When fuel prices soared during an energy crisis, Smith's company had only five thousand dollars in the bank. Investors refused to give him more money, and his company was on the verge of bankruptcy. With only five thousand dollars left, Smith went to Las Vegas and won twenty-seven thousand dollars playing blackjack. He used this as seed money, which kept his company afloat. Today, FedEx is one of the world's most valuable companies. Remember that the reward is in the risk. No risk, no reward. I'd far rather risk two or three awkward dinner parties than to endure a lifetime of bland dinner parties.

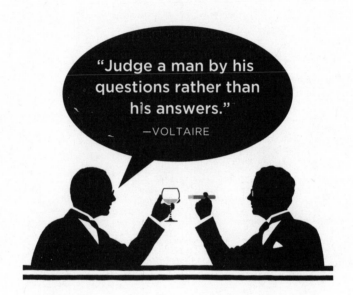

CHAPTER 1

Be
Intentional

*D*ing! Ding! Ding! The sound of my fork tapping against my wineglass rang sharp and clear over the babble of voices in the dining room. Carol and I were hosting another dinner party, which meant I was sitting in the middle of another group of gregarious guests, some of which we hoped would help us get CAbi off the ground.

Unfortunately, this dinner had started out with the same challenges as our previous encounters. The guests automatically clustered in small groups, with hushed conversation happening around different sections of the table. Everyone seemed to be talking about something inane or innocuous, such as what movie they saw last week or their plans for summer vacation. More small talk! And no one showed any inclination to go deeper.

We weren't going to give up. Instead, I started to consider how to set the table for something more than small talk. Fortunately, this time I had a plan.

Ever since my rock-bottom encounter with Julie the soccer mom, I had pondered long and hard how to improve the quality of the conversations at our dinner parties. The more I thought about it, the more I felt like the root of the problem was the lack of purpose or intentionality of our gatherings.

Each time we hosted a dinner, Carol and I expected the guests to engage in meaningful, inter-esting conversation all on their own. We were providing good food, good wine, and a stimulating environment with interesting people, and we assumed that good conversation would automatically appear—almost like it was a natural by-product of those atmospheric conditions.

Clearly, that wasn't happening.

I thought, *If meaningful conversations aren't happening organically, maybe we need to inject a catalyst of some kind.*

Before I share that catalyst, I want to focus on the idea of intentionality. Each winter, I pick a word to focus on during the coming year. A couple of years ago, I picked the word *intentionality*. If you haven't heard it before, intentionality is basically the act of being deliberate or purposeful. It's about performing actions with awareness, doing things deliberately, consciously, and on purpose. In other words, you're not letting things happen in your life by accident. Intentionality has an entirely different meaning in philosophy. I'd have to ask you to sit on my sofa to bore you with the details of that

Intentionality is basically the act of being deliberate or purposeful. It's about performing actions with awareness, doing things deliberately, consciously, and on purpose.

teaching. I chose *intentionality* because I thought I wasn't being purposeful enough with my life, and I realized that I had to make those decisions, set those goals, do whatever I wanted to do, but I was the one who had to make it happen.

Intentionality is how I came up with a solution to my dinner party dilemma. When you are seated around a dinner table, whether with family, friends, acquaintances, or strangers, chitchat is simply transactional. There's no real conversation. You're not finding out where people really stand on issues. You're not interacting. I think that dinnertime is a marvelous time for intentionality. Being intentional is not always convenient or comfortable, but neither are dull dinner parties.

That's when the idea hit me: What if I took the bull by the horns and had all of our guests focus on one idea at a time? One question at a time? Wouldn't that be a great way to cut through the small talk and open the door for real, meaningful conversation? I was about to find out.

Ding! Ding! Ding! I rang my wineglass again, then said, "Hello, everyone. I'd like to try something a little different for our time together this evening. I'm going to ask a question, and then I'd like everyone to take a turn answering it, and then we'll see where the conversation goes from there. Does that sound like fun?"

Fortunately, none of the guests said, "No." I pushed forward.

"Okay, here's the question: What was one of the most important days of your life, and why?"

For a few seconds, nobody answered. I felt like the keynote speaker, standing in front of thousands of salespeople at a big convention, who had just told an opening joke—and nobody laughed. There was complete silence, and I'll admit I started to feel a little concerned. People understandably would be hesitant to jump right into the deep end, thinking their answers were going to be corny or too personal.

But then Carol spoke up and shared for a couple minutes about the day she and I decided to go into business together. God bless my lovely and talented wife!

Carol's story seemed to break the ice for everyone else, and from that moment the group was off and running. One by one—with only a few prompts from me when necessary—each guest shared his or her answer to the central question, and the rest of the table listened attentively. Sometimes someone asked their own question or jumped in with a comment, but for the most part each person took the "microphone" for a few minutes, told their story, and then passed it on to the next guest in line.

I was quickly blown away by the response. Each time a guest spoke, he or she shared about a genuinely compelling moment from their past. Most followed Carol's example by sharing about positive events—meeting their spouse, being inspired to chase a dream, having children, finally accomplishing an important goal, and so on. But there were other stories sprinkled in about tragedy and loss, such as the death of a parent, the loss of a good friend, a serious illness, or the stress of losing a job.

When the last person had shared, I looked out across the table to see every guest smiling back at me with rapt attention.

"Well," I said, "what did you think of this little experiment?"

They loved it! Several people asked me to provide another question—which I did gladly. In fact, we spent the rest of that evening discussing more table questions.

> **Everyone at the table was involved in the conversation, everyone enjoyed themselves, and people opened up and became vulnerable in ways I'd never imagined.**

The entire experience was a smashing success. Everyone at the table was involved in the conversation, everyone enjoyed themselves, and people opened up and became vulnerable in ways I'd never imagined. It was like putting missing flavor back into food. Best of all, no small talk!

That was the moment I became a huge advocate of this conversational method called table questions—and an even bigger practitioner.

• • •

What are table questions? Well, the simple answer is that table questions are a method of convening and directing a social encounter with intentionality and purpose, rather than expecting people to engage with one another on their own. Table questions are a way of managing a conversation and moving it in the direction you want it to go. It's like being a traffic cop or the conductor of an orchestra. A traffic cop steers everyone in the right direction to avoid pileups. A conductor might not make a sound, but he or she makes everyone in the orchestra powerful through his or her actions. It's the same concept with table questions.

> Table questions are a way of managing a conversation and moving it in the direction you want it to go.

The method for using table questions is relatively simple. It starts with having someone who is willing and able to initiate the conversation—a role I call the "convener," or the host. It's the convener who identifies the topic of discussion, steps in when necessary to guide or redirect the conversation, and then either brings things to a close or asks a new question.

Once you have a convener, the only other thing you need are the table questions themselves. These are questions designed to lead people into a specific type of conversation—table questions can be fun or serious, light or heavy, quick or long to answer, and so on. And the best part is that you get to choose which type of interaction your group will experience based on the questions you ask.

In other words, you have the power!

I'll talk more about how to identify effective table questions later in this book, and I'll also share some important tips on how to serve as a competent convener. But for now, I want you to understand that table questions are an excellent way to bring life to social situations that would normally be doomed to wallow in the shallow waters of small talk.

> Whether it be a dinner party, corporate retreat, team-building activity, Sunday school, or any other social setting, table questions will make your discussions more interesting and bring you much closer to others.

Here's another great thing about table questions: they're flexible. They can be used in almost any situation where people are gathered together and expected to engage and interact with one another. Whether it be a dinner party, corporate retreat, team-building activity, Sunday school, or any other social setting, table questions will make your discussions more interesting and bring you much closer to others.

The other advantage to table questions is that they improve the odds of everybody having the same experience that evening. Without them, some guests may be engaged in an intensive conversation at one end of the table, while you or other guests may be floundering in a shallow conversation at the other end of the table. You're all at the same dinner. You're eating the same meal. Why not have everybody experience the same conversation together? You just need to be the convener of it. Otherwise it's almost like serving one person tacos, another person prime rib, and somebody else crispy duck.

I've used table questions at literally hundreds of dinner parties over the years—parties with few guests and many guests; parties with younger people, older people, and a mix of generations; parties with women, with men, with couples, and so on. But I've also used table questions around campfires and fireplaces to help rugged men interact after a long day of fishing or hunting. And

I've used table questions at both corporate events and spontaneous gatherings.

In short, just about anywhere and everywhere you'd like to see meaningful conversations and interactions between people, table questions are an amazing addition to your tackle box.

Wouldn't you like to experience a meaningful discussion the next time you gather with a group of interesting people? (Or even uninteresting people—table questions work there as well!) Just think of it: rather than settling for a bunch of surface-level chit-chat, why not take the reins with some purposeful questions? You no longer have to dread going to a dull dinner party. Instead, you could use the time you are there to really interact with your family, friends, and those you want to get to know. If you aren't intentional about it and don't direct the conversation where you want it to go, it will usually fall to its lowest common denomination, which is just small talk.

All you need to do is present an interesting topic for the group to consider, and then guide your guests in an orderly manner as they express themselves and share what comes to their minds.

If that sounds difficult or intrusive, just give it a try. Just one time! I promise, you won't be disappointed.

And the more you continue to grow as a practitioner of table questions, the more you'll have the opportunity to orchestrate your questions and conversations as you see fit. That means you'll be able to direct your gatherings toward the places you want them to go—rather than being taken as a polite but unwilling hostage to the whims of your guests!

With that in mind, I'd like to offer four guidelines you can follow to get started with table questions as effectively and efficiently as possible:

1. Plan ahead.
2. Ask the right questions.
3. Be in control.
4. **MAKE IT FUN!**

When I talk with people about the power of table questions, many times I'll hear something like this: "Well, that sounds easy. I'll just ask a question that everyone can talk about, and we'll be all set! No problem."

Yes and no. It's true that the concept behind table questions is simple, which is part of what makes them so profound. But using table questions effectively is not easy. Especially not at the beginning.

Even after decades of using table questions to spark and guide meaningful conversations, I still need to prepare in order to make sure things go as smoothly as possible. I still need to be purposeful.

The same will be true for you.

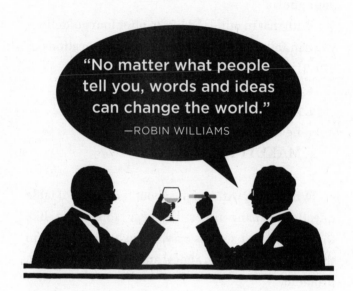

"No matter what people tell you, words and ideas can change the world."

—ROBIN WILLIAMS

CHAPTER 2

Plan
Ahead

L et's take a deeper look at that first guideline: "Plan ahead."

Many people mistakenly believe that table questions can be, and even should be, spontaneous. They believe they can wait until the salads have been served, think for a few moments, and then rattle off a spectacular table question that will keep guests talking for the next several hours.

Take it from me: that's an unrealistic expectation. In fact, in my experience, spontaneous table questions are much more likely to serve as conversation stoppers than conversation starters. (I'll share one of my own conversation-stopping moments in the next chapter.) If I'm going to host a dinner party, I can't wait until right when we sit down at the table to come up with questions—and I'm pretty creative. Instead, I start thinking about them the day before.

It can be intimidating to lead a table question discussion because you are sticking yourself out there to do so. It's like stepping onto the pitching mound for the first time, or singing a solo in the church choir. You're the center of attention and the spotlight is on you. If I don't have my questions pretty well rehearsed and hammered out, the entire dinner might pass me by, and I'll never find an opportune time to speak up. I'll miss a great opportunity—and even waste an evening of getting to know people in an authentic way.

Think about it: if you were going on a two-week trip to Europe, you wouldn't wait until the day before to get your affairs in order. You would confirm airline tickets, hotel reservations, car rentals, and dinner reservations a few weeks in advance. If you were going camping in the Rocky Mountains, you wouldn't wait until the day of your trip to make sure you had everything you needed in order: tents, sleeping bags, water, backpacks, hiking boots, food, and warm clothes. Remember what Benjamin Franklin said: "By failing to prepare, you are preparing to fail."

Indeed, it's important to plan ahead and think through several key factors in order to ensure a successful experience for both yourself and your guests.

First, you need to evaluate your audience. Consider these four key questions:

- Who will be participating in the conversation?
- What will the group dynamic be like?
- How many people will be there?
- What are they expecting?

Evaluating your audience is critical because table questions are not a cookie-cutter experience. In fact, matching the right table question with your specific guests is more like pairing a great steak with the perfect wine. You don't want to just throw things together and hope for the best!

For example, how many people are you planning to engage through table questions? If there are lots of people—more than ten or twelve—you'll need to choose questions that can be answered in thirty seconds to a minute. That way everyone will have an opportunity to speak and there will still be enough time left for follow-up comments or additional questions. If there will be fewer than ten people present, you can craft questions that allow guests to talk much longer and reveal much more about themselves.

> **Evaluating your audience is critical because table questions are not a cookie-cutter experience. In fact, matching the right table question with your specific guests is more like pairing a great steak with the perfect wine.**

If your guest list will include mostly single people, you should avoid questions on the subject of relationships— and especially questions about marriage or children. You want to avoid making people feel awkward at all costs because people who feel uncomfortable shrink away from conversations—especially deep conversations. On the other hand, if your guests will be mostly couples, it would be a great idea to ask questions that allow people to reveal details about their spouse and their relationship if they choose to do so.

Another item to think through in advance is whether your guests know each other and are familiar interacting with one another or whether they will be relative strangers. How well do they know each other? If your guests are friends or acquaintances, you'll have more freedom as the convener to ask questions that are more personal or require deeper thought. If your guests are just meeting one another for the first time, you'll want to stick with questions that are more general and don't require a lot of back-and-forth conversation.

Informational questions are a good way to start because when you are sharing information, that's a lot less threatening. For example, if there are couples at your dinner who don't know each other, you would say, "Tell us a little bit about yourselves and how you met your spouse." That's safe for them. It's informational and sort of superficial, yet everybody's talking.

The main idea here is to make sure you have thoroughly evaluated who will be participating in your guided conversation. That way, you can ask questions that will be fun and interesting to that specific group—rather than stick your foot in your mouth.

Second, you need to plan ahead for table questions by determining where you want the conversation to go. In the same way that it's important to know who will be talking together, you also need to decide ahead of time what you want the group to talk about.

Here's another way of stating this idea:
- What's your goal for the conversation?
- What are you hoping you will experience?
- What are you hoping your guests will experience?

Ultimately, you want to get to the point where people feel free to open up about their personal opinions, situations, feelings, hopes and dreams, or whatever you intend to elicit from your question. But you don't want to make that seem forced because that creates awkwardness. You need to be what I call a subtle convener. If you make it too obvious, it's just rote. It will seem stiff and won't feel natural.

For example, think back to the CAbi dinners I hosted with my wife that I mentioned earlier in this book. We had a specific goal for those dinners: we wanted to identify women who had leadership qualities and could be a good fit for our new business. Therefore, it was important for me to identify that goal ahead of time and plan out my questions accordingly.

I draw from my vast experience as an entrepreneur in stressing that this step cannot be skipped. We've all been asked what we do for a living, and every entrepreneur knows what comes after their response to that age-old question: "Wow, it must be so nice to work for yourself."

I can't tell you how many family members, friends, and strangers have said that to me verbatim. Yes, the flexibility and self-sufficiency of working for myself have been rewarding, but it's become apparent to me how romanticized the notion of entrepreneurship is in our modern culture. Here's a little secret: entrepreneurship is just as stressful and exhausting as it is gratifying.

When you're running your own company, every second of the day is valuable. Frequent meetings, client calls, interviews, emails to answer, and other typical day-to-day tasks are just a few of the duties that take up an entrepreneur's time. With a limited number of hours in a day, successfully managing a busy schedule is contingent upon efficiency. In other words: work smarter, not harder. I modeled my time management approach after this philosophy when I was the Chairman of CAbi, and it's what I credit for the company's global success.

Whether you run a startup, a Fortune 500 company, or work in Silicon Valley, planning topics ahead of meetings is vital to success. Meetings are notorious time wasters, whether they're planned in advance or on a whim. Executives often only communicate the dates, times, and general subject matter of meetings to employees prior to the actual meeting itself. While having the event on your calendar is important for planning out that day's schedule, it's also critical to plan out the substance of the meeting as well. A lack of direction is often the main culprit of lengthy, unproductive strategy sessions.

There are good ways to avoid wasting time. To ensure brevity and efficacy, Homejoy CEO Adora Cheung has her employees add agenda topics to a spreadsheet before every meeting and then prioritizes them based on urgency. If something isn't listed, they don't talk about it. Steve Ballmer, the former CEO of Microsoft, created a spreadsheet to budget his time and to ensure that he didn't spend too much time on unnecessary things. Jeff Weiner, executive chairman of LinkedIn, makes sure he has enough time to think and doesn't spend all day reacting.

You want to be just as efficient and productive while preparing for dinner conversations that go beyond small talk.

One of the questions I asked during those CAbi dinners was, "When was the first time you realized you were a leader?" Now, obviously that question had the potential to make people feel awkward or uncomfortable if they were not leaders or didn't think of themselves as leaders. But because our specific goal in those dinners was to identify potential leaders, I was willing to take that risk.

Also, knowing my goal ahead of time helped me adjust my behavior as the host for those dinners. I wanted to see if any of our guests would step up and take on a leadership role; therefore, I intentionally stepped back a bit as the host. When the conversation lagged, I didn't jump in to help it get going again. Instead, I waited to see if someone else would notice the lull and decide to take action. Fortunately, a few women spoke up, took the plunge, and became great collaborators for us at CAbi.

There are lots of reasons to have a firm understanding of your goal for a specific get-together before you begin asking table questions. Let's say you are gathering with a group of people you hope will become friends and socialize together on a regular basis. In that case, your goal for the party is to help your guests get to know one another and to help them connect in a meaningful way. That goal should influence the questions you ask and the way you function as the host.

In such a setting, it would be best to ask several questions designed to have shorter answers. That way, your guests will have the opportunity to share a lot of information about themselves, and also to learn much about everyone else. It would also be a good idea to help those guests interact with each other as much as possible. Make it known that it's okay for participants to ask each other questions after someone shares an answer, or give opportunities for people to respond. "What does everyone think about the story Jerry just told?"

A few of the questions you might ask in this particular situation include:

- What is your favorite book to read? Why?
- What was the last movie you watched? What did you think?
- What is your favorite sport to watch or play?
- What kind of music do you listen to? Who are your favorite performers?
- Where does your family like to vacation?
- What are your hobbies?
- What are your favorite foods?
- What is your most cherished family tradition?

Obviously, you wouldn't be scratching too far below the surface with these introductory questions, but that's exactly the point. You're attempting to offer these people, who might have been strangers before they sat down at your dinner table, an opportunity to get to know one another. What are their commonalities and differences? Are there enough similarities for them to interact beyond your dinner? While it's too early to know if they can become close friends, they can begin to determine if they have shared interests and opinions, which might plant the seeds of a relationship in the future.

Now, you might be thinking, *What if I don't have any agenda or goal for my gathering? What if I just want to get some people together to have fun?*

Well, that's great! In such a case, "having fun" is your goal. And that's a wonderful goal! I host many dinners and other get-togethers for no other reason than to enjoy the people I enjoy. Life is what you celebrate. A little party never hurt anyone. But you still need to plan ahead.

Specifically, when you want to lead the table discussion in a way that generates fun, you'll want to focus on questions that are light—maybe even a little rowdy if you know your guests can handle it. And as the host, you'll want to be less involved in "managing" the conversation; let people run wild a little bit.

> You're attempting to offer these people, who might have been strangers before they sat down at your dinner table, an opportunity to get to know one another.

- What did you want to be when you were a kid?
- What's the craziest thing you've ever done?
- If you had to pick one—skydiving, bungee jumping, or scuba diving—which one would you choose? Why?

- What's the most embarrassing thing that ever happened to you at work?
- What would the name of a reality TV show about your life be entitled? Who would play you?
- What are some of your guilty pleasures you're willing to admit?
- What's the best prank you've successfully pulled off?

Again, the goal is to have a firm understanding of what you want to accomplish when people come together; that way, you can be intentional about crafting questions and hosting your guests in a way that is likely to accomplish those goals.

Remember that there is an art to asking the right question. Questions shouldn't be closed-ended, which allow participants to simply answer yes or no. For example, let's say you asked your guests, "Did you watch the Los Angeles Rams win the Super Bowl last night?" They either did or they didn't. There are other examples of closed-ended questions that you should try to avoid that allow participants to answer with one-word or very short answers.

- Where did you go to college?
- How many children do you have?
- Do you like your job?
- How old were you when you got married?

You want to ask open-ended questions, which allow your guests to extrapolate in their answers and provide more insight and description. For example, you could word the Super Bowl question this way: "It has been so long since the Rams won a Super Bowl. What do you think it means for Los Angeles?" For the questions I referenced above, you might instead ask:

> More than anything else, keep your questions on topic and keep them short.

Where did you go to college, and what did you like about it most?

Tell me about your children. Are their personalities similar?

What is the most rewarding thing about your job?

At what point did you know you were going to marry your spouse?

More than anything else, keep your questions on topic and keep them short. There's nothing more frustrating to me than watching an interview on *60 Minutes* or the news, in which the journalist rambles on and on before he or she finally asks the question. Even the best journalists are guilty of doing it. It's like they're trying to put words in the subject's mouth, and sometimes I think they probably are. Keep your questions short and simple. Keep them open-ended. We'll get more into that subject in the next chapter.

The final step in planning ahead for a table question discussion is to actually write your questions. And yes, I do think it's important to write them down. Even if you don't bring those written questions to the actual event or conversation, the discipline of getting your questions on paper (or on a 3×5 notecard in my case) will pay dividends because it will allow you to see if you have enough questions ready or if any of your questions duplicate themselves.

> You'll never really be sure how many questions will be necessary in a given gathering, and it's far better to have too many questions than too few.

Writing table questions that actually lead to discussion and conversation is an important skill, which is why I've dedicated all of chapter 3 to that subject. So, stay tuned.

Before we finish this chapter, though, I want to offer one final tip about the amount of questions you should prepare in advance of your gathering. Specifically, it's important to write more questions than you'll need. Why is that important? Because you'll never really be sure how many questions will be necessary in a given gathering, and it's far better to have too many questions than too few.

I've found that a good table question can occupy a group of around ten people for about thirty minutes.

That means each person would have three minutes to answer the question, or each person could have two minutes with time left over for people to interact or ask follow-up questions. But remember: that's just a general guideline. Each gathering will be different.

So, how many questions will you need for your guests? There's no way to know exactly. How long do you want the conversation to last? If you're hoping people will talk for an hour and then do something else, you can probably get away with two or three questions. If people will be sitting around a campfire for hours and hours, you'll need to have a lot more questions ready.

Your goal for the gathering will also influence how many questions you need. As I mentioned above, if your guests all know each other, you can ask questions that require longer answers and more interaction—which means you'll need fewer questions. If your guests are strangers, you should plan to ask more questions.

I won't pretend that there's some kind of formula for figuring out how many table questions you'll need—although that would be nice! The key is to think through who will be attending and what you hope to accomplish. With experience, you'll learn to get a good grasp on exactly how many questions you'll need.

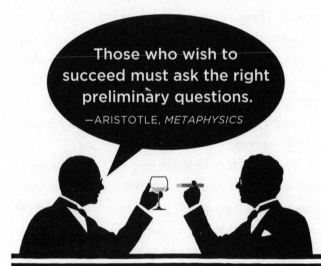

Those who wish to succeed must ask the right preliminary questions.

—ARISTOTLE, *METAPHYSICS*

CHAPTER 3

Ask the Right Questions

It was New Year's Eve, and Carol and I had invited several of our closest friends over for dinner. These were couples we had known and met with for years as part of a fellowship group, so I really wanted the evening to go well.

And it was going well. We had lobster on the table paired with a perfect selection of wine. The setting was lovely and the conversation lively. We were basking in the kind of warmth that comes from gathering with a room full of friends who know each other well and genuinely like spending time together.

Then I put my foot in my mouth. Or maybe both feet.

Ding! Ding! Ding! "Okay everyone, it's been a lovely evening so far, but what would everyone say to a table question or two?"

Our guests smiled. They all knew about my general dislike of chitchat and my fondness for table questions.

I pressed on with my first question: "What are two things you would like to change about your spouse?"

Yikes! All these years later, I still can't believe I asked that question!!! Worse, I can't believe some of our guests chose to answer it! One of those guests was my good friend Jim, who was about fifteen years older than me. My question should have sent alarm bells ringing in his head. Danger! Danger! Do not enter!

Instead, he thought for a few moments and offered what I can only assume was an honest response.

I learned later that Jim's wife didn't talk to him for two weeks after that dinner!

In all my years of using table questions, I've made several mistakes. I've asked several questions that were worded poorly or that just ended up being duds—questions that failed to get people talking in any meaningful way. Thankfully, I think that question on New Year's Eve was the only time I sent someone to the doghouse.

It was a good question, but I set it up the wrong way. You could easily flip it and make it a wonderful question by asking, "What are the top two characteristics you most admire about your spouse?"

The good news is that you can learn from both my experiences and my mistakes. Let's look together at some key guidelines for crafting table questions that lead to interesting conversation—and avoiding questions that lead to marriage counseling!

• • •

Like I told you earlier, the most important thing to remember when writing table questions is to leave them open-ended. By that I mean, make sure your questions have more than one possible answer, and try not to ask questions that are so specific they can be answered with just a word or a single phrase.

As an example of what I mean, consider the question, "What is your favorite color?" That's a closed question, as opposed to one that is open-ended, because it only has one answer: "My favorite color is green." Or: "My favorite color is blue." The last thing you want from a table question is for people to go around the room giving one-word or one-phrase answers—that is the opposite of a stimulating conversation! It's more like a lightning round of *Jeopardy*.

So, what would an open-ended question look like? For starters, you could simply add the phrase "and why" to the end of the previous question: "What is your favorite food and why?" That opens things up quite a bit, since guests can give any number of reasons why they chose a specific food as their favorite. Here are some other ways to take a question like "What is your favorite food?" and make it more open-ended:

> **Make sure your questions have more than one possible answer, and try not to ask questions that are so specific they can be answered with just a word or a single phrase.**

- When did you first discover your favorite food? *(encourages people to share a story)*
- What is it about your favorite food that makes it your favorite? *(forces guests to think critically about their preferences)*
- How does food make an impact in your daily life? *(a more provocative way to talk about the subject of food)*

Remember this little saying as you write your table questions: Open-ended questions are conversation starters, but closed questions are conversation killers. Remember that the purpose of table questions is to open up communication, to embolden relationships, or to create new ones. Ask questions that will force your guests to pause and think. They will feel important because you're interested in what they think and believe, and they'll feel valued because everyone else is listening to what they have to say.

The next guideline for writing quality table questions is to make sure they are provocative. I don't mean "provocative" in the same way that Kim

> The purpose of table questions is to open up communication, to embolden relationships, or to create new ones.

Kardashian or Miley Cyrus have been throughout their careers. I'm talking about questions that are thought-provoking. Questions that almost feel a little dangerous and have a little edge to them—but not ones that are completely over the top and will make your guests feel uncomfortable and not want to answer.

> **Table questions need to have some meat on the bone. They need to be at least a little bit outside of what people would normally talk about in a social setting.**

Another way to say it is that your table questions need to have some meat on the bone. They need to be at least a little bit outside of what people would normally talk about in a social setting. If you want to lead others into thoughtful and interesting conversations, you'll need to start with insightful and engaging questions!

In his landmark book *How to Win Friends and Influence People*, author Dale Carnegie encouraged his readers to be good listeners and to persuade others to talk about themselves.

So ... aspire to be a good ... attentive listener. To be interesting, be interested. Ask questions that other persons will enjoy answering. Encourage them to talk about themselves and their accomplishments.[3]

Carnegie wrote his self-help book in 1936. It is one of the bestselling titles of all-time with more than thirty million copies sold worldwide. More than eight decades later, his advice still rings true today. People want to be heard, they want to be asked questions that will make them think, and they want your interest to be sincere.

All of us have probably left a job interview or first date and said to ourselves, "I wish they had asked more questions." There's nothing worse than sitting through an interview or meeting and feeling invisible. It might feel like your words or actions don't matter. When you do finally speak up or get asked a question, others might interrupt you or speak over you. It might feel as if your contributions don't matter.

> People want to be heard, they want to be asked questions that will make them think, and they want your interest to be sincere.

It can feel the same way for people in social settings, and that's why table questions are so important. They encourage everyone to participate in a lively discussion. Even introverted or shy guests will want to be a part of it. If you're aware that a friend or someone's spouse might be a little uncomfortable speaking about themselves or opening up in front of others, I would encourage you to start with less intrusive or provocative queries and then escalate to more thought-provoking questions later. Use a few icebreakers to instigate conversation when someone might be reluctant.

Here are a few examples of questions that might get one's feet wet:

- Where did you grow up? What did you like about it most?
- What's your dream job?
- If you didn't have to worry about money, what's the first thing you would do?
- What foreign countries have you traveled to? Which one was your favorite and why?
- Do you like to cook? What is your favorite meal to prepare?
- Tell me about something that made you laugh this week.
- If you could invite one famous person to our dinner party, who would it be and why?

You get the idea. Those questions can lay the groundwork for deeper, more thought-provoking questions later. Chapter 12 gives you several examples of good, provocative table questions. You can select from those questions as you have a need, or you can use them as examples when you practice writing your own table questions in the future.

Finally, it's important for you to write and use table questions that are appropriate.

First, as mentioned in the previous chapter, make sure your table questions are appropriate for where you want the conversation to go during your gathering. In other words, make sure you write or choose table questions that will match your goals. If you want your guests to just have fun and enjoy one another's company, don't ask questions that are heavy or boring.

Second, make sure your table questions are appropriate in a more general sense. Meaning, make sure you're not going to put your foot in your mouth like I did when asking what my friends would change about their spouses! Don't ask single people about relationships and children. Don't ask a Democrat about Donald Trump. Don't ask a Republican about global warming and immigration. Don't ask a vegetarian about steaks. Don't bring up your love of hunting and fishing with an animal rights advocate. Unless I'm with friends from my fellowship groups, I rarely ask about religion. And never, ever ask about someone's finances. Bringing up someone's family is typically a bad idea, and try to avoid gossip at all costs. It's uncouth. Follow proper etiquette, avoid taboo topics, and you'll be fine.

To give you some examples, I never ask table questions that are sexual in nature or that pry into that aspect of people's relationships. Sure, there may be some people in your group who are willing (or even excited) to talk about the intimate details of their relationships. But most people are much more likely to shut down instead. So I avoid sexual questions like the plague.

> If you don't know how to ask the correct and appropriate question for your guests, you'll be the guy who is drinking alone at cocktail parties for the rest of your life. No one wants that.

I also try to avoid political questions in most cases—especially political topics that are already polarizing and are likely to polarize your discussion. The last thing you want at your party is a food fight!

Again, this is why it's important to know who will be attending your gathering and to decide ahead of time where you want the conversation to go. There may be times when a political question would work wonders for a discussion, if everything is approached appropriately. You have to survey the guest list and carefully analyze how it might go down before you ask a political question and step into that minefield. If you don't know how to ask the correct and appropriate question for your guests, you'll be the guy who is drinking alone at cocktail parties for the rest of your life. No one wants that.

For example, I recently hosted an event for a governor. There were about twenty people present, which was the right number for a conversation. Instead of ignoring politics altogether, I tapped my wineglass with my fork and said, "It's great to have the governor here, and we'll get to hear from him in a few moments. But first, I thought it might be fun for him to hear from us. So, let's go around the table and answer this question: What are the top attributes a public servant should have, in your opinion?" Of course, everyone was eager to share their opinions with the governor right there at the table. What could have been a boring meet-and-greet turned into a great conversation!

> No matter how much you argue and whether or not you're right, the pigeon is going to knock all of the pieces over, do you-know-what on the board, and then strut around like it won the game.

As long as you have a good grasp of who your guests are and where you want the discussion to go, you'll know whether it's appropriate to ask a political question.

The same goes for other sensitive subjects, including religion. Discussions about politics and religion remind me of the old joke about playing chess with a pigeon. No matter how much you argue and whether or not you're right, the pigeon is going to knock all of the pieces over, do-you-know-what on the board, and then strut around like it won the game. There's no way you're telling the bird it's wrong!

> **The best table questions are open-ended; they should allow guests multiple options to explore and give them the wiggle room to escape.**

In general, I think it's best to avoid subjects that are divisive. Avoid topics where people are likely to say, "I'm right, and anyone who doesn't agree with me is wrong." That's not the recipe for a healthy conversation. Some people are going to be so set in their beliefs that you're never going to change their minds. Just remember that everyone is valuable to a conversation—some when they enter it and others when they leave.

Remember that the best table questions are open-ended; they should allow guests multiple options to explore, engage, and share their stories. Great table questions should also focus on ideas and topics that everyone can participate in and enjoy without feeling awkward or uncomfortable.

For instance, a friend of mine who worked for Disney in their international film and video distribution division was a guest at one of our dinners. He was even there when Walt Disney was alive. I remember saying, "You have that great history of being there. Why don't you tell us a couple of your most memorable stories of being with Walt?" People get to hear a story that's really worth listening to. And it's honoring the person you ask to share. From that you can segue off into a question such as, "How about the rest of you? What's one of your most memorable stories of somebody you had a relationship with?"

Remember that sometimes people aren't good storytellers, so you have to help them with follow-up questions, such as, "What was the point of you wanting to tell us about that?" You need to help people at times too, because you don't want them to trap themselves.

Later in this book, you will be able to read and consider sample questions that you can implement immediately in your conversations. They will be a great guide and a helpful template as you learn the important skill of writing your own table questions.

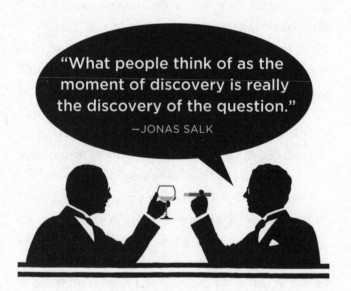

CHAPTER 4

Stay in Control

It was 1964. I was attending high school in Hins-dale, Illinois, where I grew up, and I had just watched The Beatles play on *The Ed Sullivan Show*. That was the first time the English rock band had performed live in the United States. Like most Americans, I was captivated by John Lennon, Paul McCartney, George Harrison, and Ringo Starr. Unlike most of the people watching, I knew right away I needed to do something about it: start a band, of course!

I called my friend Pete.

"Pete, I just watched The Beatles on *The Ed Sullivan Show*, and we need to start a rock band," I told him.

There was silence for a few moments on the other end of the line. Then Pete said, "But we don't know anything about starting a rock band."

"I know we don't," I said, "but nobody else does either. And this thing is gonna be big."

That week, Pete and I went out and bought guitars, along with some amplifiers and all the necessary attachments. We taught ourselves the three chords that make up most rock songs, held auditions to find a lead singer, and practiced whenever we could grab a couple hours together. "The Birds" were born. Within just a few months, we were booked most weekends and playing gigs all around our stomping grounds of suburban Chicago. I was making one hundred and fifty bucks a week and couldn't have been happier.

We later changed our name to The Hard Times, and the band broke up when Pete and I went to college. Obviously, we never made it to the level of The Beatles, or even The Oneders (if you saw Tom Hanks in the movie *That Thing You Do!*). But our band did play at some of the bigger shows in our area. And we made pretty good money for high schoolers—good enough for me to buy a classic Porsche before I went to college, which I thought was pretty fantastic.

Right now you're probably wondering, *Why is Jan telling me about his rock 'n' roll glory days from the sixties?* Good question!

The answer is that a big part of using table questions effectively is maintaining some level of control over the conversation. And the best way I can describe what that control should look like is through the metaphor of leading a band—although not a rock band. Instead, it's more like leading the kind of band that has trumpets and violins and clarinets.

In other words, when I lead a group through discussing a table question, I think of myself as the conductor of an orchestra.

What does that look like? Well, first of all, it means I try to stay out of the way as much as possible when the conversation is going well, just like a good conductor knows he or she is not the main focus of the audience's attention. The conductor is there to make sure the orchestra performs and the music sounds the way it's supposed to sound. In the same way, as the host or convener, you are there to make sure the conversation is healthy, productive, and fun. You're not there to preach a sermon!

> **As the host or convener, you are there to make sure the conversation is healthy, productive, AND FUN!!!**

As the Italian conductor Riccardo Muti famously said, "A conductor should guide rather than command."

But, just like in an orchestra, there will be times when a table discussion starts to get out of tune. There will be times when the "music" of a conversation moves away from your goals and purpose. And there will even be times when one of the "players" goes rogue and starts doing his or her own thing, which creates a cacophony rather than harmony.

Those are the situations where you need to step in and take action—when you need to "conduct" the conversation. So, let's take some time to explore how you can do that effectively.

• • •

One of the key elements of being in control during a table discussion is learning to keep track of the pacing for that discussion. And that starts with when to actually begin the conversation by introducing the first table question.

You must be patient and determine the absolute best time to introduce a table question to your guests. Interestingly, I don't introduce the first question right at the beginning of a gathering. I wait. I do this because I don't want the experience to feel overly programmed. I don't want people to feel as if they're being guided through some kind of planned agenda— even though in many ways they are. I don't want it to feel like an awkward company Christmas party they're being required to attend.

> **Be patient and determine the absolute best time to introduce a table question to your guests.**

Instead, what I like to do is allow our guests to arrive and settle in for several minutes. If we're eating a meal, I make sure everyone is served and we have time to enjoy the first course. Naturally, people will engage in small talk with one another, and that's okay. Because when I do introduce the table question, it's almost as if I'm rescuing my guests from their own chitchat. And they appreciate it!

Next, how you introduce the table question is important. You need to capture your guests' attention in a way that shows you are in control.

Have you ever been to a public event where there's an emcee who spends several minutes trying to get the attention of the crowd? "Excuse me, ladies and gentlemen. Excuse me! We're about to start, so if I could have everyone's attention, please." There's nothing worse than listening to someone banging a spoon on a wineglass at a wedding reception or party, while people continue talking among themselves. That's the opposite of being in control. That shows hesitation and weakness, which are poor qualities to display when you're trying to serve as a conductor.

When it's time to introduce the first table question, smile, relax, maintain your self-confidence, and stand up to ask the question.

How many times have you heard someone completely botch a joke because he or she bungled the delivery of the punch line? For a punch line to land with the fury of a Mike Tyson uppercut, you must punch the line a little harder and with more conviction than everything else you're saying. And you must pause slightly after delivering the punch line to give your audience time to react. In many ways, the same is true of table questions. When it's time to introduce the first table question, smile, relax, maintain your self-confidence, and stand up to ask the question.

Back when Carol and I were running CAbi, we used to have yearly gatherings with all 3,400 members of our sales team. We called those semi-annual events "The SCOOP," and it's where we conducted sales training and introduced new fashions for the next year. There were a lot of ladies in one place! One year, we even rented out the entire Opryland Hotel and Convention Center in Nashville, which was loads of fun.

During those gatherings, I never wanted any of our speakers to have the burden of begging all those women for attention, so we would always play a short video clip right before someone was scheduled to speak—something fun and attention-grabbing. And we always turned the volume way up to drown out conversations that were taking place all over the ballroom. That way our speaker could be at the microphone with everyone's full attention on them as soon as the video finished.

I recommend you take a similar approach when it comes to capturing your guests' attention. I don't recommend using a video in most cases, but I do think it's necessary for you to make a loud and clear signal that something important is about to happen. And I think it's necessary that you actively be in control—turn up the volume and make certain you're getting through to everyone quickly and efficiently. Make them want to listen to what you're about to say.

For me, the best way to accomplish that at a dinner party is to clang my fork against my glass five, six, or even ten times—whatever it takes. When I see all eyes on me, I introduce my first question. Once you have their attention, you have to figure out how to hold it. Sims Wyeth, a speech and presentations coach in New York, describes in his article "10 Ways Great Speakers Capture People's Attention" two kinds of attention: neck-down and neck-up. "Neck-up attention is when the listener has to make an effort to pay attention. Neck-down attention is when the listener is riveted to the speaker: she can't help but pay attention."

> Make them want to listen to what you're about to say.

Wyeth's tips on captivating an audience include starting with a bang, not a whimper; making what you're going to say about your guests, not you ("talk about their goals, their aspirations, their anxieties"); keep it concrete at the start by using a prop and language that appeals to their senses; keep it moving; get to the point; arouse emotion; keep it interactive ("the give and take between speaker and audience breaks through the reticence and reserve of listeners, encouraging them to engage with the speaker and play a part in the proceedings"); keep it short; and finally, be yourself.

> *Listeners interpret everything a speaker does: they read your face, your inner rhythm, your posture, voice, and stance. In fact, the human mind ascribes moral intention to physical cues having the slightest hint of emotional expression. The problem is the mind does this in a matter of seconds, and you have to speak longer than that. Plus you may be nervous, not at your scintillating best, so your technical skill at capturing and holding attention could be the difference between success and failure.[4]*

Gauge the temperature of the room and decide when it's time to move on to another question.

Finally, it's important for you as the convener to manage the pacing of your conversation by deciding when it's time to move to the next question—and when it's time to bring the discussion to a close. There's no formula you can use to decide when a question has run its course. Instead, it's something you feel.

Gauge the temperature of the room and decide when it's time to move on to another question. Let's say everyone around the table has given their answer to a specific question and nobody seems ready to jump back in with another comment or a question for someone else. You'll feel the lack of energy. You'll know it's time to introduce another question or, if the hour has grown late, bring the conversation to a close. If you don't like how the conversation is going and want to end the night early, just do what I sometimes do: I flick the lights three times to let everyone know it's time to go!

On the other hand, if you planned for a specific question to last for half an hour, but your guests have been discussing that topic for forty-five minutes and don't show any signs of slowing down, you should stay in the background and let the conversation run. Remember, there's no need for the conductor to step in when the music is flowing well. That would be like walking to the mound in the middle of a no-hitter and pulling your starting pitcher. If the fire is burning bright, there's no reason to douse it.

> **There's no need for the conductor to step in when the music is flowing well.**

In addition to controlling the pacing of your table conversations, it's also critical that you manage the participation of your guests. Meaning, you need to actively stay in control to ensure that one or two people don't dominate the discussion and make sure the handful of quieter guests at the corner of the table don't get lost and excluded. Remember that you're not there to be a teacher or lecturer. You're only a convener and facilitator whose job is to make the conversation flow better. You want to remove any obstacles that might be preventing some guests from participating, and that might mean telling an overzealous guest to zip it. (We'll get more into that in chapter 7.) The conversation will be much more enjoyable if everyone is involved. You want everyone to take something rewarding home from the table. You want them to grow from the experience.

> **Remember that you're not there to be a teacher or lecturer. You're only a convener and facilitator whose job is to make the conversation flow better.**

The easiest way to manage participation is to say, "Let's go around the table and hear from everyone." That way, you're not giving a license for over-talkers to dominate the conversation or under-talkers to hide away. You're setting the expectation that everyone will get a chance to talk. Of course, as the host, it's your job to keep track of who has yet to respond to a question, and it may be necessary for you to give a little prod here and there. Read the table and look your guests in the eyes. You might be able to discern who wants to speak up and who might be reluctant to do so. Don't be afraid to encourage someone to participate, but try to avoid putting them on the spot. Simply say, "Sally, we haven't heard from you yet. Are you ready?"

> As the convener, you should never, under any circumstances, force someone to speak or share in a conversation. That's never appropriate, and that's never a good way to treat a guest.

A lot of times people feel uncomfortable about the idea of calling on somebody or calling someone out. As the convener, you should never, under any circumstances, force someone to speak or share in a conversation. That's never appropriate, and that's never a good way to treat a guest. However, it is important that you make sure everyone has the opportunity to speak. And that's why it's necessary for you to check in with guests who have yet to share. Because sometimes people really do want to talk and have something meaningful to say, but they're waiting for permission. And you need to give it to them.

I try to make my table questions open-ended enough so that guests can give a simple answer. That in itself can be someone's own form of retreat. But there are times I remember where a simple question elicited an emotional response of tears and sobbing from somebody who needed an opportunity to open up like that. You want to make the transition from small talk feel natural, but you also need to gradually make your questions and remarks deeper as the conversation goes on.

> Sometimes people really do want to talk and have something meaningful to say, but they're waiting for permission. And you need to give it to them.

Think of the last time you went to a great movie. As the camera scenes go from the widescreen to the big landscape shot, they get tighter and tighter and tighter. And finally, they are close-up on a face or on someone's mouth or their eyes. I think that same thing happens with table questions. As you start the evening, people will make chitchat comments. They might even say things to each other on the side. But then as the evening goes on and the questions continue, everybody develops a natural desire to want to hear.

Everybody ultimately does want to open up; it's the old deal of the hide-and-seek game. A friend of mine who was a psychologist told a story about playing hide-and-seek with his son. He was finishing graduate school at the time, and they lived in a one-bedroom apartment. There weren't a lot of places where his son could hide. But the boy would hide, and his father would go around and say, "Oh, where are you? I don't know." And then he'd say, "Oh, I give up. I'm going away. I'm going to leave." And the boy would jump out and say, "Here I am!"

> **Everybody wants to be found. But society encourages us to become masters of learning how to hide.**

Well, everybody wants to be found. But society encourages us to become masters of learning how to hide. I found this to be true at my dinner parties just like it is in all of life.

The great thing about table questions is that each person participating gets to hold the microphone. Each person gets to share what's on his or her mind. For many people, your table discussion may be the first time they got to hold the microphone all week— or the first time in months! They may have been craving a chance to really share something significant about their lives—or just to be the center of attention for a few minutes.

Do your guests the honor of being in control of a healthy, productive conversation. Because the rewards really can be special for everyone involved.

CHAPTER 5

Make It Fun

According to Greek mythology, Sisyphus was a clever man. He was the original founder of Corinth, a king, and also a bit of a trickster. In fact, he was so cunning, sly, and deceitful, he managed to escape death and the underworld by fooling the gods—twice!

Sisyphus's ill deeds caught the attention of Zeus, who wasn't pleased by the idea of mortal human beings forgetting their place in the natural order of things. Zeus also didn't want others to be encouraged or inspired by this upstart trickster.

So, when Sisyphus finally died for the third time, Zeus was ready. The king of the gods punished Sisyphus by condemning him to live for eternity in a dusty valley until he was able to push a boulder to the top of a mountain and roll it down the other side—a feat that was much easier said than done.

In *The Odyssey*, Homer describes Sisyphus as literally wrestling with the boulder, using his hands, shoulders, and knees to thrust the enormous rock up the mountain slope while sweat poured from his body. Each time Sisyphus finally maneuvered himself close to the mountaintop, however, the weight of the boulder became too much. It overwhelmed him and went rolling and crashing back to the bottom of the valley. Exhausted and covered in dust, Sisyphus had no choice but to follow the boulder down the mountain, only to start the entire process over again.

Talk about a miserable routine for eternity!

I've never tried to roll a boulder up a mountain, but I have been involved in many Sisyphusian-like conversations in which I've been asked the same idle questions over and over, given the same boring answers again and again, and then repeated the process ad nauseum and ad infinitum.

That's what I mean when I talk about small talk and chitchat. It's boring! It's routine. It's the same thing over and over again, and I'm done with it. Curiosity might have killed the cat, but ceaseless chitchat drives me mad.

Now that you're nearly halfway through this book, I hope you've accepted the truth that you can be finished with Sisyphusian-like small talk as well. Using the power of table questions, you can lead gatherings and conversations that are nowhere close to boring. Instead, they can be filled with engaging subjects and tons of fun!

Laughter is one of my favorite things about table questions. I've been in some gatherings where everyone at the table was laughing so hard they couldn't breathe. Really, if I could bottle up the kind of joy I've seen people experience in those moments, I would be the most renowned doctor in the world. Because laughter and fun are so life-giving.

Doctors have often said that laughter is the best medicine. Even the world-famous Mayo Clinic contends that laughter helps us relieve stress, stimulates our heart, lungs, and muscles, relieves pain, improves our immune system, and increases our sense of personal satisfaction. I can't think of any pharmaceutical drug that does that! I've also been involved in gatherings where interesting people had the chance to go deep into their stories, and I found myself literally on the edge of my seat waiting to hear what was coming next. You know what? That's fun too. That's the opposite of boring!

As the convener of your gatherings, it's critical that you continually point your guests toward the goal of having fun. So, let's take a few moments to explore how you can make that happen.

• • •

Cyndi Lauper told us "Girls just want to have fun." And that's true of guys as well. Everyone likes to have fun! Which is why you need to make laughter a primary ingredient of any social conversation. What are some specific ways to make sure a table discussion starts fun and stays fun?

> Make laughter a primary ingredient of any social conversation.

First, you need to make sure you're prepared. And

that's really what we've been exploring over the past few chapters.

When you plan ahead to identify your goals and purpose for a specific conversation, you'll prevent that conversation from wandering aimlessly between different topics—which is no fun. When you make sure to ask the right questions by matching those questions with your purpose and your guests, you won't stick your foot in your mouth like I did when I asked my friends what they would change about their spouses. (Trust me, that was no fun!) And when you are in control of the discussion, you won't allow certain guests to kill the night by dominating the conversation or by staying inside their shells.

> **When you do a good job of preparing for a table discussion, you'll create a healthy environment for that conversation to succeed, which leads to everyone enjoying themselves and laughing together.**

This is a simple and straightforward concept. When you do a good job of preparing for a table discussion, you'll create a healthy environment for that conversation to succeed, which leads to everyone enjoying themselves and laughing together. When you fail to prepare, you leave the door open for lots of land mines to blow up in your face and those of your guests, which can be quite miserable for everyone at the table.

Next, you can keep things entertaining during your gatherings by setting the right example. Your guests will have a good time when they see you having fun!

Now, I'm not suggesting you go out and buy a clown suit before your next dinner party. Nor do I think you should watch a bunch of videos from Rodney Dangerfield in his prime so you can do a stand-up session in the middle of the meal. (Although that might actually be entertaining: "When I was a child, my parents moved a lot—good thing I always found them." *Hey-o!*). And it's probably best to stay away from the kind of crude jokes that made entertainers like George Carlin, Chris Rock, and Richard Pryor famous. That language is better for the men's locker room (or nowhere at all) and might not go over well with some of your guests.

The comedian Jerry Seinfeld famously said that there were four levels of comedy: "Make your friends laugh. Make strangers laugh. Get paid to make strangers laugh. Make people talk like you because it's so much fun." As the convener for table questions, you want people laughing with you because they're having so much fun.

People want to laugh and enjoy themselves. It's up to you to give them a reason to do so. Studies have shown that laughter releases endorphins, which makes us feel good about ourselves and others. Dr. John R. "Jack" Schafer, a former behavioral analyst with the Federal Bureau of Investigation and author of *The Like Switch: An Ex-FBI Agent's Guide to Influencing, Attracting, and Winning People Over*, wrote,

> **People want to laugh and enjoy themselves. It's up to you to give them a reason to do so.**

> *This good feeling creates a bond between two people and imbues a sense of togetherness in groups. The Golden Rule of friendship states that if you make people feel good about themselves, they will like you—and laughter does just that. It makes you feel good about yourself and the person who triggered your laughter.[5]*

Schafer found that laughter signals intelligence and produces better long-term relationships too. In order to set the right example, you should do everything in your power to set the right mood for your guests. That starts with being a warm, relaxed, and gracious host. Greet your guests by name as much as possible.

Make sure everyone is comfortable. And if you're hosting a dinner, do your best to provide tasty food, good wine, and an engaging atmosphere.

> Even taking notice of someone's posture and facial expressions will give you an idea of who might be a willing participant and who won't be.

Before everyone arrives, create the right ambience with lighting and music. Welcome your guests with a smile. It might be a good idea to use place cards to avoid awkward moment when it's time for your guests to sit down to eat. By creating a seating arrangement, you can position talkative guests on opposite sides of the table to keep them from dominating the conversation. The same goes for quiet ones. Remember that every great dinner party begins and ends with the spirit of the host.

At many of my dinner parties, I like to have people to serve the meal and wine. This helps eliminate distractions and allows my guests to focus on the conversation. Obviously, not everyone can afford to have servers at their parties. I would suggest having your children serve the meal, or find a couple of teenagers in the neighborhood who would be happy to do it for a few bucks. I try to do everything I can to create an environment where my guests feel like they have my complete focus and nothing is distracting.

It's also a good idea to "read the room" before starting table questions. Who's sitting next to whom? Who's smiling and who isn't? Even taking notice of someone's posture and facial expressions will give you an idea of who might be a willing participant and who won't be. If you're familiar with some of your guests or if they're returning participants, it might be good to ask for their answers first. They've participated in table questions before, so they have an idea of what's coming. It always works better than asking someone who has never been a part of the experience to jump right in and be the guinea pig.

Another way to "read the room" is to observe your guests as they're mingling and chitchatting. What's the mood in the room? Who seems to be engaged in conversations and appears to be truly interested in what others are saying? Who showed up early and who was late? That might be a sign of how much they're looking forward to the experience you're about to give them. Try to identify body language that indicates boredom or excitement. The people smiling are the ones who will probably be your best participants. They can't wait to sit down and have fun!

Setting the right example also means showing guests the correct way to interact with one another, especially when answering or discussing a table question. For example, it's critical that you never, ever treat someone poorly or rudely after they answer a question. Never put someone down for what they've shared, even if what they said was nonsensical or strange. Why? Because not only will you make that guest feel insulted, you'll put everyone else on notice. You'll make everyone at the table think, *I better be careful what I say, or I'll get zinged as well.*

> Someone once said that sarcasm is a lot like jazz—it's hard to identify but you'll know it when you hear it.

In the same way, I think it's important to avoid sarcasm when you're leading a discussion. Someone once said that sarcasm is a lot like jazz—it's hard to identify but you'll know it when you hear it. Sarcasm isn't as much about the words you choose as the tone with which you say them. Never use a sarcastic tone—in most cases. If you're familiar with all your guests and you've been friends for a long time, you'll have enough relational equity to joke with them and maybe be a little sarcastic. But in most situations, sarcasm puts a negative spin on a conversation, and that's exactly what you want to avoid. Some people might feel nervous about saying something that could earn a sarcastic comment from you, and it also gives other guests permission to respond sarcastically themselves.

Do everything you can to avoid negative communication when you're convening a table discussion. That includes put-downs, sarcasm, rolling your eyes, and so on. Try to avoid crossing your arms while others are talking, and don't sigh in the middle of someone's answer. Those are signs of rudeness.

On the other hand, you should actively set the right example by being encouraging and supportive in your speech. When someone digs a little deeper to answer a question in a way that's especially thoughtful, reward them for it. "Wow, Stan, I think what you just shared is really important." Or, when someone decides to share after being hesitant to talk for the first part of the gathering, offer some encouragement. "Jane, I really appreciate you jumping in there. You always add a lot to the discussion."

> You set the right example for your table discussion by being the ideal participant.

Basically, you set the right example for your table discussion by being the ideal participant. If you slouch down in your seat and play with your food after you introduce a table question, you'll give people the impression you don't really care about what your guests are saying in their answers. On the other hand, if you maintain eye contact with your guests and actively show them you're interested in what they have to say, they will feel welcome to engage on a deeper level. And they'll be more likely to treat their fellow guests the same way.

Another important part of being a fun host is making sure that your guests, who might not know each other, are comfortable engaging with each other. Talking to someone you've never met before is uncharted territory. For many people, it's difficult to do. For some, it can be downright intimidating. We've all probably endured awkward conversations with strangers that feel forced and uncomfortable. As we engage with a friend of a friend we've never met or attempt to converse with a complete stranger at a dinner party, our palms get sweaty, our blood pressure spikes, and we start fumbling our words.

When that happens, the worst fears flow through our minds: *Am I boring him? Is he even listening to me? I must sound like a fool.* Then comes the awkward silence. You can't wait for the conversation to end. To prevent this from happening, make sure to introduce your guests to each other if they're not already familiar with each other, and keep your

> **Be genuine. Be warm. Be kind. In other words, be fun!**

table questions fun. Don't make the conversation too serious until your guests have had the opportunity to get to know each other.

Most importantly, be enthusiastic as the host of your table conversation. Be genuine. Be warm. Be kind. In other words, be fun! As a result, you'll increase the level of enjoyment experienced by both yourself and your guests.

Finally, you can keep things fun during your gatherings—including while you're doing table questions— by nipping problems in the bud. I don't want to give the impression that table questions are a panacea for social gatherings. Sometimes things will go off track. And in those moments, you as the host and convener have the power to make things fun again by recognizing potential trouble spots and steering the group toward safer ground.

> As the convener for a table discussion, there are times when you need to be more than a conductor of an orchestra. Sometimes you need to be a lifeguard at the pool.

As the convener for a table discussion, there are times when you need to be more than a conductor of an orchestra. Sometimes you need to be a lifeguard at the pool. Sometimes you need to actively intervene in order to keep a conversation fun and positive rather than allowing it to turn sour.

For example, let's say a guest is struggling to find the right words during his answer to a table question. He's trying to tell a story, but he's starting to wander, and you can tell he's feeling frustrated with himself. There's a lot of potential awkwardness in a moment like that. A lot of opportunities for something to go wrong.

What would you do in that situation?

If it were me, and I felt like the guy really was about to hang himself out to dry, I would step in with a lighthearted comment. "Well, Roger, I like what you've shared so far, but let's hear from your wife now and get the right answer." Something like that. Again, it's important not to be mean-spirited or rude. But there's value in helping someone who needs help. And if you don't do it, who else will?

On the other hand, it's important that you try not to interrupt others. It happens to the best of us. Something that we feel is important pops into our head and we don't wait for the other person to stop talking before we blurt it out. But we need to be careful not to interrupt because it's rude and might give the person talking the wrong idea that you don't respect them or care about what they have to say.

I'll give some other examples of potential problems and how to solve them in the next chapter. But the basic idea here is that one of your roles as the leader of a table discussion is to keep things positive by identifying trouble spots and helping everyone steer clear of them. That's a valuable contribution to any conversation.

Remember, everyone likes to have fun. So don't be afraid of fun! Lead your gatherings in a way that gives everyone the permission and freedom they need to enjoy themselves, and you'll be well on your way to a fantastic experience—not just for your guests, but for yourself as well.

If table questions aren't fun, your guests might feel like Sisyphus ceaselessly rolling that rock up and down the mountain in the underworld. And that isn't much fun!

PART II

Identifying Trouble Areas

On April 13, 1970, astronaut John "Jack" Swigert delivered words from space that NASA's mission control never wanted to hear.

"Okay, Houston, we've had a problem here."

Swigert and the other Apollo 13 astronauts had just heard an oxygen tank explode aboard the spaceship *Odyssey*. Two days into their mission, they had to abort their lunar landing and figure out how to get home safely. There was concern in Houston that the carbon dioxide the astronauts had expelled from their lungs would eventually kill them. On top of that, they had lost two of three fuel cells. Without them, the spacecraft wouldn't have enough power to return to Earth.

Demonstrating incredible ingenuity and problem-solving skills, Mission Control engineered a carbon dioxide filter from materials on board the spaceship, including duct tape and a cue card from the flight manual. The astronauts were told to change their course and go around the moon in order to gain gravity that would slingshot them back to Earth. Even more daring, the astronauts were told to use the Lunar Module, which was supposed to have landed on the moon, as a lifeboat to get home. Miraculously, with tens of millions of Americans watching on TV, the astronauts safely splashed into the South Pacific on April 17, 1970.

Looking back on all the dinners and events Carol and I have hosted over the years, we could have used Swigert's now-famous line for most of them. That's not because of a lack of planning, and it's certainly not from a lack of skill or ability—not on Carol's part, at least!

No, it's a simple fact that when you invest your time, talent, and treasure in any venture that's worthwhile, you can expect a little trouble. And sometimes it's a lot of trouble. To offer just a few examples, Carol and I have been forced to work through food that wasn't prepared, guests who failed to show, chairs and other equipment that broke, speakers who ran late—and that doesn't even include the rivalries, feuds, grudges, and spats that can be common whenever you ask a bunch of people to gather together.

> **When you invest your time, talent, and treasure in any venture that's worthwhile, you can expect a little trouble. And sometimes it's a lot of trouble.**

Basically, if you can think of something that could go haywire during a social gathering or a table discussion, I've probably experienced it in one form or another. Thankfully, that means I'm well equipped to offer you some potentially useful advice!

In the pages that follow, you'll find a number of common problems or scenarios that often threaten to hijack or derail what should be a happy, healthy conversation. You'll also find my best solutions for those problems, which I sincerely hope will give you a leg up when you're tempted to put a palm to your forehead and say, "Houston, we've got a problem!"

CHAPTER 6

Stay Out of
the Way

I t's a common misconception that all conversations are supposed to be balanced in terms of
participation. This is especially true with table
questions. New hosts and conveners often believe
that every guest should talk the same amount—that
everyone should have the same size slice of the
conversational pie.

In reality, that's not the case. People have
different personalities and different experiences,
and everyone prefers to share in amounts that make
them individually comfortable. Some people enjoy
talking more; others prefer talking less. You'll actually
be creating more problems than you solve if your goal
as a host is to divide up a three-hour dinner party so
that each of your ten guests talks for exactly eighteen minutes. Remember that
fairness isn't everyone getting exactly the same
thing; it's everybody getting what they need.

> **Fairness isn't everyone getting exactly the same thing; it's everybody getting what they need.**

Instead, your primary goal should be to make
sure that everyone has an equal opportunity to join
in the conversation. That being said, there will be
times when one or more people dominate a discussion to the point of causing a problem. And when

that happens, you as the convener need to step in and resolve the issue.

Many conveners don't feel comfortable addressing an over-talker. It feels too much like conflict. I understand the hesitation, but remember your role as the conductor of your table conversation. When the tuba section gets out of control during a concert, the maestro needs to signal them to quiet down for the benefit of everyone else involved. It's part of the job description, right?

Now, you don't have to be mean or abrasive when you address someone who is dominating the conversation. Many people talk too much not because they are arrogant or pompous, but because they sense a gap in the conversation and they want to fill it. Some people are described as compulsive talkers. "Compulsive talkers seem to overvalue the quality of their contribution and signal (through refusal to listen) that others' ideas are unimportant," wrote professors Robert N. Bostrom and Nancy Grant Harrington of the University of Kentucky in their

> When the tuba section gets out of control during a concert, the maestro needs to signal them to quiet down for the benefit of everyone else involved.

report *An Exploratory Investigation of Characteristics of Compulsive Talkers*.

> Worse, they often seem unaware of their problem. Regardless of cause, there seems to be universal agreement that talkers are a problem, both to themselves and to others. Accordingly, information about talkers would be useful in helping talkers control this behavior.[6]

You should be as subtle as possible in your corrections as the conductor. I want to emphasize again that your main job as the conductor of a table question is to stay out of the way. Yes, you want to be in control during each discussion—but being in control doesn't mean being the primary person who is talking all the time. It just means making sure the conversation is moving along in a healthy and fun way.

Your main job as the conductor of a table question is to stay out of the way.

Being attentive is a key part of knowing when to step in. I've used the conductor analogy, but another way to think of it is like this: You're like a bus driver. And your job is to get everybody in the right seat and to get the bus to where it's supposed to go.

If you just listen, you could let someone dominate the conversation. One of the reasons people talk too much is their fear that they're actually not being heard. In these cases, it's important to engage with them and ask them questions to help them "land the plane," as they say. After you've done that, if they're still circling the airport and going on and on, set a time boundary by saying something like, "You've only got a few minutes until it's the next participant's turn." It might take a little while, but I promise they'll eventually find the runway.

> You're like a bus driver. And your job is to get everybody in the right seat and to get the bus to where it's supposed to go.

Most importantly, be polite, even as you're trying to steer them along. You don't want to be rude. Instead, you want to be graceful to them, but you need to get them to stop talking to give somebody else a chance.

How should you do that? Good question!

You can look for a pause in a person's dialogue and then jump in with, "That's a great point, Mike. I really appreciate you sharing it. Jim, we haven't heard from you yet. What's on your mind?" In the vast majority of cases, Mike will catch your hint and correct himself without any conflict or any need for a dramatic showdown.

As I mentioned in a previous chapter, you should start by giving one or more subtle notices that the person in question is hogging the conversation. "That was a great story, Bill. Thank you. Okay, let's keep things moving so that everyone has time to share—who hasn't given their answer yet?"

On most occasions and with most people, taking these steps will solve the problem. But as you've probably heard, "most ain't all." You may encounter a situation where someone either misses the hint or straight out refuses to be quiet.

If that happens, your next step is to see if you can talk with the person privately. You might encourage everyone to take a break for five minutes to stretch their legs, make a phone call, or use the restroom. Then, take the over-talker aside and share your concerns. "Bill, I'm not sure if you're aware, but you are really dominating the conversation right now. Could I ask you to help me get others involved?"

If that doesn't work, or if you don't have an opportunity for a private chat, then you need to address the situation directly during the discussion. I know that will sound difficult for many people, but as the host of the conversation, it's your responsibility to create a healthy environment. And if you've noticed Bill dominating the conversation, it's safe to assume the rest of your guests have noticed it as well—and they probably feel as uncomfortable as you do.

So, get out your elephant gun and take care of things. "Bill, I'm going to ask you to pause right now so that we can hear from those who haven't been able to share yet. We'll get back to you once we move to the next question."

Don't be rude about it. Don't be snarky or sarcastic. But do be clear, and do be direct. That's the only way to kill the elephant in the room.

What about the other end of the spectrum? What about a situation where a guest refuses to share his or her answer to the table question or refuses to join in the conversation?

You don't want this to become uncomfortable for you, that individual, or your guests. And since this is likely to happen, you need to be prepared to take the next step without it becoming a moment of embarrassment or a moment of regret.

Remember, your job as the convener is to make sure that each of your guests has the opportunity to engage in the discussion and join in the conversation. But if someone refuses that opportunity—whether they decline to answer a question or even choose to sit out the entire event—you've done your job.

But let's back up a bit. For numerous reasons, you can't push a person. Let's delve into some of those reasons so that you will be able to enter into this situation recognizing that their refusal to participate may not be related to anything you are or aren't doing.

Their personality may make it difficult for them to even step into the room. A guest who is a strong introvert could likely be already *so* outside of their comfort zone that anything else would be the push they cannot handle. They could have internal walls up all around their introverted heart and one night isn't going to tear those down. They dread small talk. In a *HuffPost* story, introverts who provided comments in a Facebook community said things like:

> **Introverts don't just dread small talk. Often, introverts *hate* small talk.**

"If it's something with total strangers, I can usually talk my way through it because it's all shallow pleasantries (although I'll still need a nap later and probably won't leave the house for days afterwards)."

"I usually try and find one person that I can talk to all night if I have to be there all night. If not, I leave after I've had my fill."

"I'll find a large-ish group that I can sit with and listen to, or maybe one close friend I can talk with. After a while I need to go off on my own, though. And I can never go out two nights in a row. I need a day to process everything."[7]

These comments and many others that pop up in stories and books about introverts reveal that it's possible, despite all of the host's best efforts, that someone may not want to participate in a social situation. Introverts don't just dread small talk. Often, introverts *hate* small talk. However, that doesn't mean that someone who is an introvert is also going to *hate* Big Talk. In fact, what you are doing could open their eyes and minds to a new way of approaching gatherings like these. It may not happen overnight, but you can make things more comfortable for introverts if you consider your approach.

A blog piece published by the University of Virginia School of Law noted,

> *Being an introvert doesn't mean you don't like people. Being an introvert doesn't mean that you don't have deep and meaningful relationships. Being an introvert doesn't mean you aren't outgoing in the right situation. Being an introvert just means that you prefer socializing differently than extroverts. Typical introverts like to spend social time with small groups rather than large ones, which may feel overwhelming and draining to them. They also tend to want to discuss "real" issues rather than making small talk. Introverts value deep relationships rather than more shallow relationships with a wider network of casual*

friends. Big events with a lot of people exhaust
them. A cocktail party can seem like a nightmare,
but a small dinner party sounds great.[8]

Whether or not someone is an introvert, extrovert, or ambivert, there are other factors to consider. Your table questions of the moment may be hitting on a touchy subject, even if it's something you think is benign. In an effort to move away from small talk and to keep things from becoming dull, maybe you've hit a nerve you didn't even know you would be hitting. And your guests aren't likely to tell you—and if they do ... well, that's a subject for the next chapter!

Frankly, you don't know what type of day an individual has had before they arrived at your event. They may have a sick child, parent, or pet, and they have spent the day caring for those individuals with little focus on themselves. You don't know what other hardships they may have endured. Life just may be bad for them right now, and showing up to your gathering was a big step for them. They may be frustrated in their career, stressed about a job hunt, or trying to figure out their next phase of life. They may be harboring bitterness toward someone in their life, and it is eating away at them.

They may have spent months alone or in mostly virtual conversations during the pandemic—or during or another time in their life that resulted in having more solitude—and just are reentering a more social period and are a bit self-conscious. Or they may be excited about something that is happening or on the cusp of happening in their life and don't want to jinx it or tell people before others know. They may not be feeling one hundred percent but may be unsure why. You just don't know how or why someone may be reacting internally to what someone else is saying.

Your next step requires you to, as previously suggested, "read the room," observing how your guests are reacting to certain questions as well as giving them the opportunity to participate. Yes, you should make sure that person knows they have permission to speak.

> **You need to bring your delegating skills to the conversation in an empathic yet direct way.**

It's similar to what I learned as an entrepreneur in terms of knowing how to delegate certain responsibilities. Delegation, when done right, frees an entrepreneur to focus on growing their brand rather than focusing on day-to-day tasks. If you attempt to do everything yourself, your business will suffer. The same concept applies to social situations. You need to bring your delegating skills to the conversation in an empathic yet direct way.

In this case, you could simply say something like, "Rob, I don't think we've heard from you yet. Would you care to give an answer?"

This may give Rob a sense of comfort to speak up.

"Deep down, people want to feel they've been heard. They will if you let them talk," authors Rico Gagliano and Brendan Francis Newnam wrote in the *New York Times Magazine*. They added that people "care about what they have to say."

> **Your ultimate goal is to get people to open up to whatever level they're comfortable with.**

Gagliano and Newnam, who host *The Dinner Party Download* podcast and radio program, also suggested in their *New York Times Magazine* column that you should never assume anything: "Asking questions can get a guest to reveal something fascinating about herself. But a quick way to prevent that is to give her possible answers. 'Why did you quit law school—*was it too boring?*' Leave out the guess. A short question is more likely to provoke details."[9]

What I've found valuable in dealing with reluctant guests is to suggest at the end of the night that they try using table questions at home. As the convener, your ultimate goal is to get people to open up to whatever level they're comfortable with, whether it's about their personal opinions on a particular subject or situation, sharing their feelings, or whatever you're trying to get at. You can actually facilitate everyone at the table becoming a convener by just saying, "When you go home tomorrow and your family is getting ready for dinner, it might be fun for you to do table questions with your children."

By doing this, you're giving your guests the opportunity to practice table questions in a place where they will feel comfortable. Then, when they come back to your next party, hopefully they'll be more willing to open up after taking that first step and practicing at home.

Remember that not everyone is going to be willing to take the leap. If your guest passes or declines, then move on. The last thing you want to do is try to force someone to do something they don't want to do. Let's say you've tried everything. Someone still won't speak up. Here's exactly what you should do in that situation: nothing.

CHAPTER 7

Set the Ground Rules

One of the hazards of introducing complex topics to interesting and passionate people is that their discussions can sometimes become a little heated—or very heated. Or even nuclear!

Several studies conducted during the past two years have shown that America is more divided than ever, especially when it comes to politics and social issues. A February 2022 poll by Georgetown University found that 70 percent of respondents believed the country was headed in the wrong direction, while 29 percent thought it was going in the right direction. Of course, there was much greater divide among Democrats and Republicans, with 87 percent of Republicans saying our country was trending downward and 55 percent of Democrats agreeing.

Whether it's because of misinformation, social media, or cable news, Americans are more divided than ever when it comes to the economy, race, gender, politics, and just about everything else in between. It's no longer just Republican versus Democrat or urban versus rural. Family members, neighbors, coworkers, and close friends can't seem to get along while discussing important subjects. Facebook has become a battlefield. Twitter has become a toxic debate floor—even in 140 characters or less. Family holiday dinners have become the scenes of bitter shouting matches.

Our discussions about the truly important parts of our lives—religion, politics, and everything else that influences us—have become so polarizing. We're just chanting our positions nowadays and not interacting. It's sad.

Unfortunately, the same land mines might be lurking at your dinner parties. Sometimes, the discussion of potentially touchy subjects, such as politics, parenting, money, religion, justice, sports teams, and so much more, can become a full-fledged argument of dividing discourse—even among nice people.

> When people are so divided, I believe talking and listening to others, especially to those people who might have opposing views, has never been more important.

That doesn't mean you should try to avoid these kinds of discussions at your gatherings. For a very long time, religion and politics were taboo topics in polite company, but not so much anymore. When people are so divided, I believe talking and listening to others, especially to those people who might have opposing views, has never been more important.

Celeste Headlee, an award-winning journalist and bestselling author of *We Need to Talk: How to Have Conversations That Matter*, says it's time for

Americans to "get over our discomfort and wade in" to these kinds of difficult discussions.

Look around your neighborhood, your city, your state, your nation, and the world," Headlee wrote. "I'm not so naïve as to believe that conversations can solve the world's problems, but I can say with confidence that not having those conversations will make those problems significantly worse. So we must begin to talk and—more important— listen to those who disagree with us on refugees, online privacy, taxes, religion, and everything else. We must have conversations, so we can eventually reach a compromise.

Headlee says it's important that you never go into a discussion trying to educate someone else. You should listen with an open mind, show respect, and stick it out, regardless of how uncomfortable it might make you feel. Go into a conversation with the understanding that there isn't going to be a winner or a loser. If it's done right, everyone is going to win because you're going to learn so much about the other people at the table and the topic you're discussing.

When a conversation becomes awkward or difficult, work through it," she wrote. "Don't crack a joke or change the subject; just work through the awkwardness. Keep going through the fog, because the light is bright on the other side. It can be tempting, as soon as someone expresses a strong opinion—whether it's on abortion or immigrants or civil rights—to test the waters with a comment or two. If you find the water too hot, you yank that toe out and run from the room. But the most important conversations are those that people are the most passionate about, those that people are the most emotional about. They are messy and frustrating and even uncomfortable, but they're also often worth it.[10]

Lay the ground rules and explain your motives before asking the questions.

As the convener of these kinds of discussions, you must first understand that certain people might be easily offended when it comes to certain sensitive topics. That's why I can't overstate how important it is to have parameters and boundaries in place if you're going to engage in these kinds of discussions. Your intention as the convener is not to fan any flames, but it's important to have a plan in place in case an argument breaks out so you can get the gathering back on track in a peaceful way.

Before you start your table questions, guests must know that they need to control themselves and avoid heated conversations that might damage relationships. It is a good idea to lay the ground rules and explain your motives before asking the questions. Let your guests know that you're not trying to disprove people's opinions about certain topics or change anyone's mind. Reinforce to them that your hope is that the exercise will lead to robust, healthy discussion that will give everyone a greater understanding of each other and the topic at hand.

> I would never want to throw out a question that puts someone on the spot or makes them feel awkward.

These are some of the ground rules I employ: Remind your guests that they're all friends, and it's everyone's responsibility to behave and have respect for other people's perspectives. Explain that they're there to share views, not to convince the others that their opinion is right. There should be no shouting or interrupting. No one is allowed to belittle, disregard, dismiss, or minimize the beliefs or opinions of someone else. Let them know that they can ask questions, but they cannot judge others or attack them with foul language. It's a dinner party, not a pro wrestling match. It's probably a good idea to limit the amount of wine you're serving on these nights to avoid loose tongues.

As you consider what ground rules you might set for your dinner party, let me warn you that everyone might not have the stomach or patience to referee these kinds of conversations. Generally, avoid topics that could push your guests to arguments or aggression. Even lifestyle and cooking websites include these same tips. In fact, one website called TheRecipe.com suggests,

> *As a general rule, controversial topics such as abortion, politics, religion, and the like are surefire ways to start fights or unintentionally antagonize your fellow guests and the host. Given how passionate people become when such topics are brought up, it's wise to not mention them whatsoever.*[11]

As you weigh the pros and cons of having these discussions, think about all of the scenes from movies and TV shows in which heated arguments have broken out at a dinner party. The repercussions are enormous, emotional, and exhausting. It happened in the 1966 film *Who's Afraid of Virginia Woolf?* and even in animated movies such as *The Incredibles* and *Shrek*. There were cringeworthy dinner party scenes in popular TV series like *The Office* and *Friends*. They're almost a nightly occurrence in many of the reality TV programs that are so popular nowadays. I'm sure you've seen plenty of these arguments if you've spent any time watching TV or streaming services, and you're probably more than aware of why you might not want to experience something similar.

But remember what Headlee wrote, "We'll never come to a common ground and mend the wounds in our society if we don't talk about the things that make us uncomfortable." Some people might not be willing to jump into these kinds of conversations, and that's okay. I would never want to throw out a question that puts someone on the spot or makes them feel awkward. I'd prefer to give them the freedom to expose as much or as little as they want to about certain topics.

A study by researchers at the University of Texas Center for Media Engagement describes animosity across political and social groups as "one of the most pressing problems of our time." The study suggests employing five main strategies when engaging in political discussions: focus on the people, not the politics; find common ground; stick to the facts and avoid confrontation; be an advocate rather than an opponent; and, finally, pick your battles.

"Another aspect of this strategy, according to our interviews, is not taking comments personally and not defining people based on their political beliefs," the researchers wrote. "By separating people from their political views, our participants reported that they could see past differences and focus on shared humanity."

Other important findings from the University of Texas study included the discoveries that "participants also sought to elicit empathy for their beliefs from those who disagreed with them by sharing stories of their own experiences," and "explaining a hypothetical situation can sometimes help people see a viewpoint they would not normally embrace."[12]

The emergence of an argument is another situation where you as the convener need to step in and address things directly. Why? Because arguments are not conducive to a healthy discussion, nor are they fun (for most people). Keep calm when tensions arise. Take a deep breath. Control your emotions. Your guests are going to feed off how you react when someone raises his or her voice or says something outrageous or controversial, so you have to be very careful about how you respond.

Keep calm when tensions arise. Take a deep breath. Control your emotions.

If things begin to get heated at the table, try to calm things down with responses such as, "Can I interrupt? We need to talk about XYZ." If someone is going on and on about their feelings about a particularly sensitive topic, you might say, "I see that this is a topic you feel very strongly about. Maybe it's time for Phil to offer his opinion about it." It's probably a good idea to go back to the most levelheaded person at the table. If you reach a point where someone is becoming too emotional and is on the brink of losing it, maybe you need to give everyone a break by saying, "I hate to interrupt you, Joan, but I have to use the restroom. Hold that thought."

> **As the convener, you have to know when to end the discussion.**

When I searched online for the phrase "ending and solving arguments," a very long list of phrases and words popped up in the Macmillan Dictionary online. It is fascinating because so many of them are relevant to what you may feel and experience as a host when this situation emerges—phrases such as "be caught in the middle," "bury the hatchet," and "keep the peace." There are nouns such as *bridge-building, conciliation,* and *fence-mending.* There are adjectives such as *conciliatory, peaceable,* and *peace-loving.* There are verb phrases such as *call off* and *pull apart.* Those don't even include the more formal words and phrases such as *arbitrate* and *settle accounts.*

As the convener, it's your job to do all of that. I usually say something along these lines to try to de-escalate the situation: "Well, we've clearly established that the two of you have differing positions on this issue, and I don't see us resolving anything this evening. But let's see what others have to say about our original question, which was . . . ."

You can also put your own spin on Headlee's advice by saying, "It's starting to feel argumentative, so I'd like to change the topic. But I want to thank both of you for talking about it." Headlee also wrote, "It can be scary to discuss our opinions with people who disagree, so it's best to thank those who take that brave step."

As the convener, you have to know when to end the discussion. If things get too heated, change the subject or bang your fork on a wineglass and end the night. Extend a thank you for everyone's willingness to discuss and engage in a difficult topic. Express gratitude that you've learned so much about the subject from their experiences and opinions and that you truly appreciate their openness, honesty, and authenticity.

Take it from me: the last thing you want to do is try to serve as a referee or moderator if things get worse. Don't try to get in the middle of an argument and help those involved find common ground or a resolution of some kind. Instead of restoring a healthy environment for healthy discussion, you'll just be feeding the argument.

To put it simply, when things get too heated during a table conversation, you need to throw water on those involved. Not gasoline.

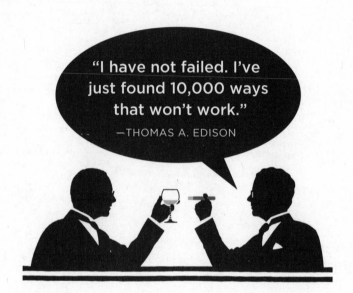

CHAPTER 8

Prepare for Failure

If you put in the time and effort to plan ahead where you want your discussion to go, think about who will be participating, and write thoughtful questions based on those factors, you usually find success with the questions you produce. Usually. But there will be times when a question is dead on arrival. However, if you're prepared for the chance of that happening, you won't be horrified if or when it does. Instead, you'll be equipped to move forward and get things back on track.

You'll know a question has bombed by the way your guests respond. Specifically, you'll feel the lack of any energy in the room. A few people may make an effort to share an answer, but it will be half-hearted. People will have trouble making eye contact with you and will instead look down at their plates or stare out across the room. Awkward silence abounds. You may feel like playing the crickets sound effect. People may excuse themselves from the table and even take a while to return. There's always the inevitable nervous transition (How about the weather? Wasn't that appetizer/ entree/dessert good? Isn't this a pretty place?) that threatens to circle back to simple small talk. The lull in conversation may cause people to turn to their phones, hoping to distract themselves with people from afar instead of engaging with the individuals sitting right in front of or beside them.

Have you ever found yourself in that kind of situation? I know I have!

You as the host may start to wonder if you're actually good at any of this. You may start to break out in a sweat, voice some type of nervous laugh, bite your nails, or do a number of other things that show you are starting to get worried and are afraid you're losing control of the situation.

There are two ways you can respond when a table question lands with a thud. The first is to try and salvage things by restating the question in a different way. Maybe your guests didn't quite catch what you were asking the first time around, and maybe hearing a similar question from a different angle will jump-start both their brains and their mouths.

As authors Rico Gagliano and Brendan Francis Newnam wrote in "10 Tips for Fascinating Table Talk at Your next Dinner Party": "To ensure that a guest's story becomes truly interesting, just ask two questions over and over: what and why. What exactly happened? What did that feel like? Seek emotional specifics. And then: Why? Why is this anecdote important? This is where the guest's most thoughtful connection to a story lies."

Let me take a moment to connect this situation to my own experience in the business world and how I've rethought the concept of "ready, aim, fire" as an entrepreneur. When a situation arises, it's an entrepreneur's goal to resolve it as quickly as possible. This aptitude for quick-thinking should be ingrained into their time management skills and can be beneficial when it comes to readapting an outlook or strategy when faced with a crucial decision. However, this hurried response to a situation is often problematic. It leads to blurred conclusions where critical details and opportunities are missed, and it creates unsustainable solutions. It also causes rifts to form between an entrepreneur and their team due to miscommunication and misinformation. The same can happen in a situation when you are using table questions.

> I don't believe in the "ready, aim, fire" business approach that so many entrepreneurs buy into. Instead, my focus is on "ready, aim, aim, aim."

For this reason, I don't believe in the "ready, aim, fire" business approach that so many entrepreneurs buy into. Instead, my focus is on "ready, aim, aim, aim." When patience is at the forefront of your professional philosophy—and your personal interactions at a dinner party—it encourages situations to move at a pace that breeds positive outcomes. Once you truly recognize the old adage that good things take time, you can fully flesh out an idea—or a question or conversation—rather than rush its time-line. The period of time between when a situation occurs and when a solution is actualized is the most important; decisions made during this time are the difference between growth and failure. The wait is worth the reward.

While a prolonged timeline can be difficult to stomach during a tight dead-line or particularly trying quarter in the business world, patience can really change one's entire demeanor. It forces entrepreneurs to take a step back and refocus on achieving their intended goals. It fosters persistence and flexibility. Once entre-preneurs abandon the idea that they can control an outcome, the delayed success that comes from waiting for the best solution is more satisfying than when the outcome is forced. Forcing your hand or someone else's hand will only result in loss—whether it be the loss of clients, contracts, employees, or the entire namesake of your company. Employing

> **The period of time between when a situation occurs and when a solution is actu-alized is the most important; deci-sions made during this time are the difference between growth and failure. The wait is worth the reward.**

this same concept in the manner in which we have discussed for this book can do the same thing and help ensure that your gatherings are memorable ones that people want to return to. Being patient may take some practice before it's perfected, but you only stand to gain from making it a virtue.

> Being patient may take some practice before it's perfected, but you only stand to gain from making it a virtue.

Your other option for dealing with a failed question is to abandon ship and start over with a new question. This doesn't mean defeat. It just means that you are prepared. But it's important that you remain in control throughout the process. You need to acknowledge that the question was a bust, then actively lead the group in a new direction. It will require humility and honesty and a bit of humor. When you do this, remember to refrain from blaming anyone in the room, which could be disastrous.

Sometimes, just to break the ice, I'll say, "Have we done this question before?" And sometimes the answer is yes! The more experience you have with table questions, the greater the risk of repeating yourself. In that case, I just throw out a self-deprecating remark or two, and we move forward.

In most cases, I find it helpful to offer a little honesty when a question bombs. Humility can go a long way and even provoke new questions for guests to ask you or for you to ask guests. I'll say something like, "This has happened to me before. I come up with these questions ahead of time, and I feel like this one maybe missed the mark a bit. No worries, though. What do you all think? Should we move on to a different question?" Then, if I get any kind of a head nod or positive response, I keep everything moving along by jumping right into my next question.

> Humility can go a long way and even provoke new questions for guests to ask you or for you to ask guests.

Remember when I said earlier that you never know how many questions you'll need for a gathering, so you should always write more questions than you think will be required? The scenario I just mentioned is exactly why it's good advice. And in the following chapters, I list dozens and dozens of questions to ask for any occasion. But even if you follow my advice and do all of the necessary planning and organizing, you still may encounter situations where you have extra time to fill and no questions to fill it with.

After all, nobody's perfect!

Once again, this is an issue I've experienced several times.

One way to avoid this is to prepare a few "of the moment" questions that you can use if you run out of your go-to questions that you think will work best with your guests. Rico Gagliano and Brendan Francis Newnam suggested in the *New York Times Magazine* that you look at the news headlines and features or even odd science articles that people may not know about. Then you can ask something unconventional but conversation-provoking, such as, "Did you know that music is beneficial to cats undergoing surgery? Or that there is a library in Norway that is amassing 100 never-before-read books that no one can check out for 100 years?" The odder, the better, it seems, because it causes a reaction—people wonder and become curious.

> Most situations can be resolved if you're willing to speak honestly, be humble, stay flexible, and remember to keep things light and fun as much as possible.

You also could do what a story in a *Quartz* article called playing "For It or Against It." [13] That's where you bring up a trend, activity, or product and ask people to say whether they are for it or against it. It should be something offbeat or neutral, not a hot-button topic or issue, the article suggests. It's similar to what you see on social media apps where people post a "this or that" photo that lets people choose instantly what they like to do (hiking or swimming?), what they like to watch (superhero movies or romantic comedies?), what they like to eat (steak or salmon?), what they like to drink (coffee or tea?), and many other things.

More often than not, I've found that the best solution is to acknowledge that you've run out of questions and to be honest about what happened. Again, humility can lead to a win-win situation. For example, you might say, "Wow, we have really been moving fast in our conversation tonight. In fact, we've moved so quickly that I've run out of questions! So I'm going to ask for your help."

That last part is important. In general, I don't recommend trying to come up with new table questions on the fly—especially if you don't have a lot of experience creating them. While you may luck your way into a great question and a great discussion, the chances are better that you'll rush into a mediocre question with a mediocre response. Or worse, you'll rush your foot right into your mouth!

To prevent this from happening, I always like to ask my guests for help. I'll say: "Here's what we're going to do. Let's go around the table, and we'll each give a topic that would be interesting to discuss. And when we get to the end, we'll take a vote on which topic to choose. Does that sound fun?"

And that's exactly what you do. Have your guests take turns coming up with an idea for a discussion topic—you may want to write them down if you've got a lot of guests—and then hold a vote. Once you know the topic, it will be much easier to come up with a question on the fly. And even if you can't identify a usable table question quickly, you can just ask about the topic in general: "Okay, the winning topic is teenagers. So, what comes to your mind when you think about teenagers? Jen, let's start with you."

● ● ●

I know it's easy to think that none of these problem-atic situations will happen to you, but as you continue to use table questions, there's always a chance that things won't go as planned and these challenges will pop up. I've shared my suggestions based on liter-ally decades of experience using table questions and hosting meaningful discussions. The tips have traveled around the world with me, from the West, where I earned my bachelor's degree in psychology from Colorado State University in Fort Collins, to journeying all over the world with Carol for CAbi and meeting frequently with vendors in Europe and Asia. So I know they really do work! It always helps to learn some troubleshooting tips because, although you can be prepared, you'll have a calm way to proceed if any of these challenging situations happen, whether it's someone talking too much, someone refusing to participate, an argument breaking out, a question failing, or the host running out of questions.

Of course, you'll probably encounter other problems that aren't listed here. Maybe even some real whoppers! But the good news is that most situations can be resolved if you're willing to speak honestly, be humble, stay flexible, and remember to keep things light and fun as much as possible.

PART III

Putting It into Practice

One evening at a restaurant in Cameron, Montana—which is the local watering hole and gathering place where we live—I ran into John Kornman, a retired U.S. Army Colonel. John served three tours of duty in the Iraq war. In retirement, he became a field trial dog trainer. John lived just downstream from us on the Madison River, where he trained and kenneled twelve top field trial yellow Labradors.

We could have settled for making small talk at the restaurant. It would have been easy to talk about the weather, fishing, or a myriad of other nonsignificant topics. Instead, our conversation that night led to a decision that would have a significant impact on my life and would bring such joy!

In our conversation, John told me that he had one exceptional pup left from a recent breeding. I should grab him before he's gone, he said. Later that night I told my wife about this new pup, and she said, "We have two dogs already, and you want a third...are you crazy?"

Even though she had said no, I called John and asked him if I could have Champ for a couple of days, and he said sure. I knew if I could get that puppy into Carol's hands, we'd have three dogs. And guess what? Yep, in a couple of days, we had three dogs!

Champ is now five years old and in the prime of his life. He is a strong, 70-pound bundle of unrestrained enthusiasm, but he follows commands like a West Point graduate. If Champ can listen well, why can't humans? He loves to fetch bumpers (his field trial training) and dives into upland bird hunting with the passion only a bird dog can express. He has unlimited energy, exhibits unrestrained joy, possesses explosive speed, and has a strong desire to please.

There have been eight dogs in my life, including Champ. Most of them were bird dogs of varying degrees of competence. Champ is super loyal, obedient, and a very loving and sensitive dog. So, for me, all that makes him the best dog in the world! I can't say enough to extol the virtues, attributes, and qualities of who I think is the world's greatest yellow Labrador: Champ! And just think, it came from turning small talk into Big Talk!

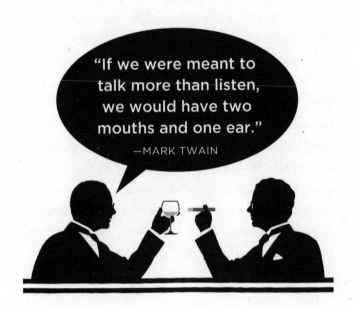

CHAPTER 9

Lead by Listening

I would be remiss to not specifically address listening. I have referenced listening and its importance in my stories and tips throughout the book, but before you move on to learning about different types of table questions, let's pause for a bit and consider the value of listening—for you and for your guests!

You and your guests are coming to this moment after being on their devices and halfway listening to the most important people in their lives, or being on Zoom meetings and partially listening while working on other tasks or even watching something that's way more interesting than the point of the meeting. It's like everyone is tapping on a mic and trying to get attention, but the pull of screens is too strong. We are all distracted by so many other things to listen to in our lives that simply trying to listen may be a huge challenge. But if you as the host fail to listen—or simply haven't developed strong listening skills—you won't be able to fully accomplish what you want to during the evening and won't help turn small talk into Big Talk.

> The musicians are communicating with each other, with the conductor, and with their audience, and everyone has a role in listening.

Let's go back to my analogy of being a conductor. One of the conductor's roles is to listen to the different musicians and instruments and guide them in the roles they play as part of the group. It's not enough to just be leading; you have to be listening too.

"The best conductors are the best listeners," Tom Service, a journalist, music critic, and author of *Music as Alchemy: Journeys with Great Conductors and Their Orchestras*, told the BBC. "They become a lightening rod of listening; a focus so that the players and the conductor can become something bigger than all of them—than all of us—at the same time as feeling fully realised as individuals." [14]

> **Conversations have rhythm and flow, and people play different roles in the rhythm and flow.**

I've never been a conductor, but I would imagine that as the musicians practice or perform, the conductor tries to identify who is out of tune, who is slower than the beat, who is faster than the beat, who is louder than needed, who is softer than needed, and a myriad of other things that could impact how the orchestra sounds as one. It's a dizzying amount of listening! As I explained earlier, the conductor is there to make sure the orchestra performs and the music sounds the way it's supposed to sound.

The musicians are communicating with each other, with the conductor, and with their audience, and everyone has a role in listening. "Live music is a celebration of listening, and a celebration of togetherness," explained Mark Wigglesworth, an international conductor, in a column for *The Guardian*.[15]

As you listen to the conversation happening around you, you also can identify who is out of tune or who is simply not getting the point of what you are trying to do. Conversations have rhythm and flow, and people play different roles in the rhythm and flow. You can identify who is slower or faster than the beat of the conversation, and in this case, it doesn't mean it's a bad thing. Instead, you may have to adjust your expectations for the questions or for the evening to take in the personalities and rhythm of those around your dinner table or campfire.

Some people may be louder (drums! horns!) or softer (clarinet! bass!) than needed in their actual volume, so you will have to gently prod them to speak up or lower their voice a bit. It's like if the oboe section of an orchestra gets too loud, the conductor has to quiet it down. Or if the tuba soloist keeps playing, you don't want that to stretch for thirty minutes because it doesn't fit into the overall symphonic performance. The first few notes are intriguing, but after that, people want to listen to the other instruments and how they play as a unified body.

But, just like the dramatic pause in an orchestra's performance, you don't need to fear moments of silence. Sometimes you are listening for... nothing! Pauses in a conversation or discussion may be necessary for people to think about what they want to contribute next or to ponder what's just been said. Those pauses may seem uncomfortable, but in actuality, they are playing an important role.

> **Pauses in a conversation or discussion may be necessary for people to think about what they want to contribute next or to ponder what's just been said.**

"Silences aren't as long as you think they are," Bernardo J. Carducci, Ph.D., director of the Shyness Research Institute at Indiana University Southeast, in New Albany, Indiana, said in a *Real Simple* story. "Remember that if you say something, the other person may need to process it. Think of silence as a transition." [16]

Speaking of shyness, Jessica Hagy, author of *How to Be Interesting (In 10 Simple Steps)*, described it like this for the *Splendid Table*: "Listening is a key way to not only take interesting information that you can share later, but to make other people feel interesting themselves. To coax people out of that shyness, just keep asking them questions." [17]

According to Ximena Vengoechea, author of *Listen Like You Mean It: Reclaiming the Lost Art of True Connection*,[18] creating a listening mindset requires using empathy, curiosity, and humility. I hope you have already seen those three traits on display so far in this book (with more to come)! Vengoechea also writes that "staying present is essential for *empathetic listening* to occur, the kind of listening where we are able to connect beyond the superficial, to a deeper, more meaningful, emotional level with others."[19]

The physical act of listening with your ears also connects to listening with your eyes, that is, showing in your own body language that you are listening to them and also viewing their own body language. A study called "Active Listening" by researchers in the health care and technology sectors gives valuable information that applies to conversation on all levels: "A person's body language can show their true emotions on the subject matter even when their words may be saying something different. Some body language examples include walking abruptly away after receiving or giving information, rolling of the eyes, sighing, shaking heads, lacking eye contact, placing hands on hips, and having a rigid posture."[20]

I've also heard the following advice many times: The next time you are in a conversation, look at your feet. Which way are they pointing? If they're pointing at the person you're talking to, more than likely you are engaged in the conversation and interested in what they're saying. If they're pointed away from that person, your feet may be giving away your true intentions that you want to walk away.

Even the way in which your toes are pointing could be a telling factor, especially if others in your group are savvy about body language. Point your big toes away from each other instead of having them both point inward. Doing little things—like being aware of how your feet are positioned and what they may be silently saying—and making simple adjustments to be more intentional about listening to those around you helps you become a better listener. And with this knowledge, you'll be able to spot what other feet in the room are telling you too!

How else can you show with your own body language that you are listening? Follow this smart list of tips from Carol Kinsey Goman, Ph.D.,

> **Doing little things—like being aware of how your feet are positioned and what they may be silently saying—and making simple adjustments to be more intentional about listening to those around you helps you become a better listener.**

author of *The Silent Language of Leaders: How Body Language Can Help—or Hurt—How You Lead.*[21] She narrowed the steps to these tips, and I've elaborated on them:

- *Nod or tilt your head.* These more innate body movements show you are invested in the conversation and are agreeing with or comprehending what the other person is saying. It offers them positive feedback.

- *Lean forward.* You may be in a louder place and need to lean forward to show the person you are talking to that their words are important. You want to hear all of their words and not miss a moment.

- *Turn your torso to make eye contact as you face someone directly.* It's the same concept as the feet in terms of demonstrating to that person that you are fully committed to the conversation.

- *Uncross your legs.* This act shows that you are not closed off to the conversation.

- *Open your arms with your palms exposed or resting on a table.* Unclenching your hands in this way shows that you are open to new insight and perspectives. It's like when kids are encouraged in school not to cross their arms in order to seem receptive to what they are being taught.

- *Hold your hands at waist level, compared to higher.* Some people may bring into the room the perception that if people hold items up high, they are showing they are more insecure. Bringing your hands and also anything else that you are holding, to waist level can indicate that you are self-assured, and people may be drawn to that.
- *Lean in, not backward.* Leaning backward could give the impression that you are looking for a way out of the conversation. Some people also may think that leaning backward is showing dominance, which may keep them from feeling comfortable answering questions.
- *Mirror another person's gestures and posture.* Although you don't want to seem like a mime, doing this in a natural and authentic way can give people a boost of confidence and also reinforce their feeling of being valued.
- ***SMILE!*** If you're in the midst of doing the table questions, simply stopping and smiling may be the toughest thing to remember to do. You may have to write a note to remind yourself to smile or ask someone close to you to signal a reminder in a subtle way.

I can't stress enough the impact a smile makes, especially if your guests are experiencing table questions for the first time. Goman explained it this way in a piece for CBS News, and it's so encouraging that I'd like to share it with you:

> *A genuine smile not only stimulates your own sense of well-being, it also tells those around you that you are approachable, cooperative, and trustworthy. A genuine smile comes on slowly, crinkles the eyes, lights up the face, and fades away slowly. Most importantly, smiling directly influences how other people respond to you. When you smile at someone, they almost always smile in return. And, because facial expressions trigger corresponding feelings, the smile you get back actually changes that person's emotional state in a positive way.*[22]

If you are just asking the question and then planning the next question as people are talking, you are missing out on being in touch with what is going on around the table or the campfire.

Another way to recognize the importance of listening is to think about, yes, politics! Imagine that the president comes to your town. You decide to go to the event and get to meet the president. You wait and wait, and then, when it's time, the president shakes your hand. And then...he or she moves on to the next person. What you really want to do is tell the person what you're thinking about how the country is being run, what you think its biggest issues are, and even how good or bad of a job they are doing as president. What he or she should be doing as a wise leader is listening to what you're saying. Because that is going to be the president's barometer as to whether he or she is in touch with what's going on throughout the country. This person could be the perfect president, if they used those opportunities to really listen.

Now, I know we all have different views on politics, including your own involvement in them. Maybe you've thought about running for office at some point, or you may even be an elected official. Maybe you would never want to be in politics, at any level. But the same concept of having a barometer for how the evening is going is worth considering. And the key way to do it is to listen to what people are saying in how they do or don't answer the questions. If you are just asking the question and then planning the next question as people are talking, you are missing out on being in touch with what is going on around the table or the campfire. And the wonderful thing is, if you follow the guidance in this book, this type of listening is not a waste because it's not small talk!

CHAPTER 10

25 Strong Opening Table Questions

To get you started, here are a series of questions for you to consider as your table questions, depending on your audience. They include questions I have used, along with questions from other sources, such as those used by researchers from the State University of New York at Stony Brook, the California Graduate School of Family Psychology, University of California, Santa Cruz, and Arizona State University in a 1997 study on interpersonal closeness. With each one of these, I've provided a glimpse into why they are strong opening table questions as well as the types of answers you could expect to receive.

I invite you to also use these to spark table questions of your own. Be as curious and as creative as you want to be!

1. What is your favorite topic to talk about? Why?

This can open up a world of conversation in that you never know what somebody might say. It could be anything from current events to history to a favorite movie to maybe a current relationship. It spices up what could have been a boring or typical conversation.

2. What was one of the most important days of your life?

This answer could run the gamut from happy to sad, from big moments to small moments. Births, weddings, trips, anniversaries, deaths, successes, and perhaps even failures could be among the answers as your guests open up and share.

3. What was one of the most surprising days of your life?

Someone's answer might bring up an idea that leads to a compelling topic for everyone to discuss. Just one person's answer could open up a whole new realm of conversation that engages everyone at the table.

4. What would you most want everyone to know about you?

The most talkative people might want to say, "Everything!" while the quieter guests may struggle to come up with something to share. This question could result in laughter as well as tears.

5. What was the most memorable gift you have ever received? Why?

This question could have people going way back to their childhood or referencing a gift they received just the other day. Be prepared for people to respond with tangible gifts as well as intangibles, such as a piece of advice from someone or simply the gift of time or the gift of love.

6. What gift(s) did you receive on your last birthday?

You will likely get more specific answers than the "most memorable gift" question, which could lend greater insight into someone's personality. You also may find that it's a way for them to celebrate and thank the gift-giver, who may also be at your table.

7. What was your favorite present you've given someone? Why?

This question also will provide a way for you to learn about your guests' personalities. You'll learn who the givers are (hint: they are probably the ones who handed you flowers, candy, a candle, or cocktail napkins when arriving), and you also may quickly discover the cheapskates at your gathering.

8. What is your favorite memory? Why?

Your guests may have a go-to answer to this one that they've used at many other parties, job interviews, and social gatherings. But some could be stumped because they have never been asked a question like this before. The responses could be detail-filled or short and vague, simply depending on what people actually remember.

9. What is your most cherished family tradition?

I'm always intrigued by these answers and how they can bridge generations! These answers can reveal everything from sweet, simple moments to extravagant adventures, all of which give you and your guests more insight into the individuals around your table and what they consider to be the most important people, things, and traditions in their lives.

10. What is your favorite holiday? Why?

Not everybody will default to Christmas. Don't be surprised to hear stories about the Fourth of July, Thanksgiving, Easter, Halloween, or other holidays that don't always mean a day off from work. This question also will reflect generational and cultural perspectives in how people describe the holiday's meaning to them at this point in their lives.

11. What is your favorite book to read? Why?

This should create automatic connections among your guests who will perk up when hearing certain titles or authors that are familiar to them. It's also a way to swing back around to a guest in another question, if you can connect that question to the book or author they mentioned in their answer.

12. What is your favorite sport to watch or play?

This invites people to talk about something that could be chitchat but on a deeper and more intentional level. The answers may be obvious to people if someone has already mentioned their hometown or college but also could be ultra-revealing as your guests learn about other people and how they spend their time and money either supporting a team or playing a sport.

13. Who is your favorite mythical being? Why?

Move over, Thor. This one may stump some people or have them thinking about who they've seen on the big or small screen—or what they remember from high school or college mythology classes.

14. What is your favorite place in the world? Why?

You will likely hear everything from exotic locales (maybe they'll also share photos!) to the simple joy of being at home in the responses to this question. As your guests listen to others' responses, they may find commonality with people across the table that then spurs them on to more in-depth conversation, such as discussing a well-known attraction or a small, intimate cafe that both of them remember. It could also inspire a discussion about the best places to stay or savvy ways to travel to that destination.

15. Where does your family like to vacation?

This is another variation of the favorite place question that invites people to share locations that are meaningful to them—and quite possibly, the memories that accompany them. This question elicits more than a list of cities and countries. Instead, it opens the conversation to discussing what makes a destination something that people want to return to again and again.

16. If you had to move, where would you want to move to?

This is another question that may result in different answers based on people's stages of life. Those in retirement who now are living in the city, state, or country of their dreams may not be able to think of anywhere else they would want to move to, and that's OK! Others may open up about places where they dream of living, such as near lakes, mountains, or beaches. You may even have someone who connects their response to plans for their next career step.

17. What would constitute a "perfect" day?

This question may conjure visions of Instagram posts showing a perfectly placed cup of coffee, a book, and a view of the mountains or water. The overachievers may talk about a business deal or promotion, followed by a swanky meal, then driving home in a Rolls-Royce that they then never have to return. Others may envision themselves surrounded by family and friends in their favorite place. It all depends on what the word "perfect" means to people and their current perspective on life, which is what makes this a "perfect" question to consider using.

18. What do you feel most grateful for in your life?

These can range from one-word answers (health, money, peace, God, etc.) to elegant expressions about people, religion, careers, hobbies, and a myriad of other things that allow people to reflect on their lives. This is another question that can bring about tears or laughter, depending on the answers and the personality of your guests.

19. What are your two favorite hobbies?

It is worth asking this question because the answers could explain why people may talk more in other questions. It also could help you determine if there are common threads among your guests and, if so, which questions to proceed with during the evening—and when to throw them a curveball.

20. What do you remember most from the last time you spent a prolonged amount of time outside?

This question may catch people off guard but it can result in simple and beautiful answers about everything from nature to key moments in someone's life, such as watching a major sporting event to cheering at their grandchild's Little League game. You'll get a sense of how and where people commune with nature as well as with others.

21. If you could invent a new ice cream flavor, what would it be called and why?

You don't have to save this question for dessert! Food often gets people talking, but this one helps you and your guests see who is the most creative in the bunch. If this question doesn't immediately work, you could start by asking people what types of ingredients they would love to see in ice cream (yes, even corn on the cob, Cheetos, and bleu cheese), then move on to making up inventive names.

22. If you could gain a new quality or ability, what would it be?

This is a "super" question that may have people channeling their inner Iron Man or thinking about the abilities of their role models and people they want to emulate. You may hear everything from the unattainable (such as running faster than a speeding bullet) to genuine desires, such as being more caring or being able to better sense the needs of others.

23. If we could add someone to the table as a dinner guest, who would you want that to be?

The answers to this question could be ultra-personal if people refer to past family members, as well as intellectual, quirky, or just plain odd. This is a question where people may build on the previous answer, or they may try to be more outlandish than the person before them. And be prepared to have people explain some of the individuals they mention—not every answer may be a recognizable name!

24. What was the best part about today?

Hopefully they'll say right now! But these answers can also give you an idea of how to proceed with the conversation as you hear about key moments that led up to where guests are now. Listening well to the responses can help you tailor the experience to your guests and show you if there's anything you need to avoid asking them.

25. What do you think about table questions?

Ask this one with your defenses down! You may be in a place where you're convinced that table questions are worth it, and no matter if people respond in a positive or negative way, it won't impact you. But if you are just giving table questions a try, this may make you question the process. Keep an open mind, embrace the effusive responses, and take any criticism as constructive and helpful.

CHAPTER 11

More Sample
Table Questions

W e're not done! Those opening questions are just the start. To follow up on chapter 12, here are hundreds more sample table questions, covering a variety of areas and topics to help you prepare and plan for every occasion. These questions pave the way for everything from straight-forward, quick responses to thoughtful, deliberate answers that reflect on individuals and humanity. As with the questions in the previous chapter, some of these are questions I have used, and others are ones that the researchers on interpersonal closeness included in their study, as well as interesting ones I've found offered by experts.

25 Questions about Culture

1. Which do you enjoy most: movies, theater, or TV? Why?
2. What is the best movie or TV/streaming show you have seen in the past month?
3. Which do you prefer: a play or a concert? Why?
4. What is the last play or concert you saw?
5. What is the most powerful communication medium, in your opinion?
6. What is your favorite news site, newspaper, or magazine and why?

7. Who do you think are the top three musical groups in the world right now?
8. What is your favorite song and why?
9. What is your favorite car and why?
10. What is your favorite movie and why?
11. What is your favorite streaming show and why?
12. Who is your favorite actor and why?
13. What is your favorite book and why?
14. Who is your favorite author and why?
15. What book has influenced your life the most?
16. What genre of book do you read the most?
17. What genre of book do you read the least?
18. What scene from a book, movie, or play do you remember the most and why?
19. What is the best restaurant you've been to recently?
20. What is your favorite food?
21. What is your most memorable meal?
22. If you could have dinner with anyone alive, who would it be?
23. If you could have dinner with anyone dead, who would it be?
24. If you were to write a book, what would it be about?
25. If you could be an animal for a day, what would you be? Why?

25 Questions
about Happiness

1. How do you describe happiness in your life?
2. Between money, sex, and power, which is your kryptonite?
3. What is more important: money, power, or health?
4. Is it better to look good or to be happy?
5. Is it better to be rich or to be happy?
6. Is it better to be powerful or to be famous?
7. How does your job make you happy?
8. Other than what you are currently doing, what would be the perfect job for you?
9. What are three things you do that bring you joy?
10. What is the most important lesson to learn in life?
11. What is one thing you have changed in your life that brought you happiness?
12. What are the three most important jobs in our culture?
13. What are the three best words to live a good life by?
14. Whom do you make happy?
15. What is one way you hope you are making the world a happier place?
16. What do you want your legacy to be?

17. What is the moment or thing that made you the happiest as a child?
18. Do you feel your childhood was happier than what other people experienced? Why?
19. Who in your past demonstrated happiness the best?
20. Who is your role model for happiness?
21. What is the most important aspect of life?
22. Do you think there is a particular time in life when people should be happiest? Why?
23. How hard is it to achieve happiness?
24. Do you think there is something after this life? Why?
25. What do you think is the secret to happiness?

25 Questions
about Love

1. What is your best description of love?
2. What are three words to describe love?
3. Why is love important to you?
4. Where does love rank in importance among these five things: career, family, money, health, and love?
5. Do you think love is an emotion or a decision? Why?
6. Have you ever felt loved?
7. When did you feel most loved?
8. How is love expressed to you?
9. What is your favorite love song?
10. Where have you seen love displayed by others?
11. What role does love play in your life on a regular basis?
12. How do you express love to others?
13. Can love be willed, or does it just happen?
14. What is the most important aspect of love?
15. Can love be lost, and can it be regained?
16. When did you love the most?
17. In what time of your life did you most find love?
18. Is it hard or easy to love? Why?
19. Do you think people can fake love? If so, how?
20. What makes love genuine?
21. Does love require sacrifice? How?

22. Do you love your family members because of who they are or despite who they are?
23. Can you love an intangible object?
24. What is the biggest lesson you have learned about love?
25. What would you like to teach people about love?

25 Questions
about Values

1. Do values matter, and if so, why do they matter?

2. Are values arbitrary or flexible? Explain.

3. Do values change with time, or do they stay the same?

4. Do values change with different relationships, or do they stay the same?

5. What are the most important values in life for you?

6. Who instilled the most important values in your life?

7. Are values universal or individual? Explain.

8. Are values cultural, or do they supersede culture?

9. What emphasis does our culture place on values?

10. What is the most important way values are demonstrated in your relationships?

11. What is the most important way you demonstrate your values?

12. How do values relate to your upbringing?

13. How did your parents teach you values?

14. How are you instilling values in the lives of your children?

15. What do you value most in someone?

16. What do you value least in someone?

17. How important of a value is trustworthiness to you?
18. What are the most important character values to you? What values do you think are necessary for someone to be a good human being?
19. What are the most important work values to you? What values do you think are necessary for someone to achieve job satisfaction?
20. What are the most important personal values to you? What values guide your life?
21. How would you rank these values in order of importance: humility, honesty, loyalty, and integrity?
22. Which value or values have you strengthened in your own life in the past year?
23. How do you demonstrate or hope to demonstrate the value of empathy?
24. How do you demonstrate or hope to demonstrate the value of tolerance?
25. In what ways do you try to show compassion?

25 Questions
about God

1. Do you think that something stands behind all of creation? If so, what?
2. How do you know there is a God?
3. When do you remember first hearing about God?
4. Have you ever had an encounter with God?
5. Would you like to have an encounter with God?
6. Is there a time you believe God has spoken to you?
7. How does thinking about God make you feel?
8. If you were God, what would your first priority be?
9. If you were God, what would be important to you? Why?
10. If you were God, how would you communicate with people?
11. If you were God, how would you show love to people?
12. What do you see as God's most important attribute?
13. What do you see as one attribute that people don't realize about God?
14. How does your relationship with God impact your daily decisions?
15. What is your concept of what God looks like?

16. How does your partner's view of God impact your own view?
17. How have you explained God to a child?
18. Do you think all religions lead to the same God? Why or why not?
19. Is the world better or worse because of religion? How?
20. Do you consider yourself religious or spiritual?
21. How has God shown his power to you?
22. How do you yearn to experience God?
23. How can belief in God be reconciled with science?
24. What religious text do you trust? Why?
25. How much do you think about God?

25 Questions
about Evil

1. Do you think there is such a thing as evil? Why or why not?
2. Where do you think evil emanates or originates from?
3. What is the purpose of evil?
4. Are individuals born as evil beings? Why or why not?
5. How common is evil?
6. Do you think evil always relates to suffering? Why or why not?
7. What external elements could result in a person doing evil things?
8. Is evil something you can feel the presence of?
9. How do you think evil affects your daily life?
10. Do you think you can feel evil? Why or why not?
11. Have you ever seen evil ruin a person's life?
12. Where have you seen evil in the workplace?
13. Do good and evil have to exist together? Why or why not?
14. What separates good from evil?
15. How does evil impact the desire for something like world peace?
16. Are all humans capable of evil?
17. Do you believe that God created evil or the opportunity for people to choose to do evil?

18. How do you think there is a good God when there is evil in the world?
19. Why do you think there is evil in the world?
20. How have you explained evil to a child?
21. What can you do about evil in the world?
22. What conditions have to be in place for evil to occur?
23. Do you think evil is the absence of good? Why or why not?
24. Do you think humans have a responsibility to judge their own acts as evil or good? Why or why not?
25. How is evil a conscious choice?

25 Questions
about Careers

1. Do you think a career is a calling? Why or why not?
2. How do you know you wanted to do the career you are in?
3. What is your favorite thing about your career?
4. Did you switch careers at some point in life? Why?
5. Would you want to switch careers at some point in life?
6. How difficult was the schooling or training to be in your profession?
7. How has your career changed you?
8. What has been the most unexpected thing about your career?
9. Do you think work/life balance is real? Why or why not?
10. What is your career motto?
11. What is a key motivation in your career?
12. What gives you enjoyment in your job?
13. What has surprised you the most about your profession?
14. How does your career fit your personality?
15. How does your career not fit your personality?
16. Have you ever been in a job just because of the money? When?

17. What challenge have you overcome in your career?
18. What is a failure you learned from in your career?
19. What is one key strength you have developed in your career?
20. How has social media impacted your views on work and careers?
21. What is one piece of career advice you would give to someone seeking to enter your profession?
22. What is a career that wasn't around when you were beginning your career that you would want to do now?
23. If you could go back to school, what profession would you want to be in?
24. What is the biggest decision you've had to make in your career?
25. What is your biggest career achievement?

25 Questions
for Couples

1. How did you meet your spouse?
2. What first attracted you to your partner?
3. How has the thing that first attracted you to your partner deepened?
4. Is your spouse your first love?
5. How did your first love impact what you bring to your relationship now?
6. When did you know this was true love?
7. What is the best date you and your spouse have gone on?
8. What is a trait you and your spouse have in common?
9. What makes someone a good partner?
10. Who is your role model for having a healthy relationship?
11. What makes your relationship unique?
12. How have you helped your spouse?
13. How has your spouse helped you?
14. Are you competitive with your spouse? How?
15. How do you spend time with your spouse during the week?
16. What is one thing your spouse understands about you?
17. What is one thing you understand about your spouse?

18. What is an interest you and your spouse both share?
19. Do you prefer to have your spouse cheer you up or leave you alone if you are in a bad mood?
20. Share your spouse's top two or three qualities.
21. Share three words to describe your role in this relationship.
22. Share three words to describe who you are as a couple.
23. What is your favorite love song?
24. If you could create a Spotify playlist name for your relationship, what would it be?
25. What songs would be on that Spotify playlist?

25 Questions
for Parents

1. How do you show love to your child?
2. When is it easiest to show love to your child?
3. When is it hardest to show love to your child?
4. What is one thing you learned the most from loving your child?
5. What do you wish you would have known before you had a child?
6. What is one thing you would tell others who are becoming parents?
7. What is one area where you have become a better parent?
8. Share three words to describe your role as a parent.
9. Share three words to describe your role as a parent in ten years.
10. How is your child most like you?
11. How is your child least like you?
12. What are the most important values you learned from a parent?
13. What are the most important parenting skills you learned from a parent?
14. How do you help your child with homework?
15. How would you describe the type of parent you want to be?
16. How did your upbringing impact the decisions you make about a child's curfew?

17. How did your upbringing impact the decisions you make about a child doing chores?
18. How did your upbringing impact the decisions you make about a child's bedtime?
19. How does social media help your ability to be a good parent?
20. How does social media harm your ability to be a good parent?
21. How do you explain bad things you see on the news to your child?
22. What is your favorite fun memory with your child?
23. What is your favorite silly memory with your child?
24. What is one phrase or question your child constantly asks or has asked?
25. What is one time you felt you were successful as a parent?

25 Questions
for Retirees

1. Do you see retirement as an adventure? Why or why not?
2. When did you feel most successful during your day?
3. What was your vision for retirement?
4. How does your vision match reality?
5. How does your vision not match reality?
6. What did people tell you about being retired?
7. How does what people told you about being retired match reality?
8. What is one new skill you have learned or are learning in retirement?
9. What is one new skill you would like to learn in retirement?
10. What is one thing you miss about working?
11. What is one thing you do not miss about working?
12. Share three words to describe yourself in retirement.
13. How is your daily routine different in retirement?
14. What is one thing you have stopped doing now that you are retired?
15. What is one tip you would give someone who is about to retire?

16. Do you live where you thought you would live in retirement? Why?
17. Where would you still like to live?
18. What destinations are on your go-to list?
19. Who do you talk to the most now that you are retired?
20. What is a guilty pleasure in retirement?
21. What is the smartest step you took to be able to retire?
22. What is something you would want to change about retired life?
23. What is something you would not want to change about retired life?
24. How did a skill from your career help you in retirement?
25. What makes you happiest in retirement?

25 Questions
for Singles

1. What are you excited about right now in life?
2. What makes you laugh the most?
3. When have you felt the biggest sense of accomplishment?
4. What is one major thing on your to-do list this year?
5. What is your favorite vacation?
6. Do you prefer to vacation by yourself or with others?
7. Where is your favorite place in the world?
8. What time in your life have you have felt the most adventurous? When and where was that?
9. Who is the person you talk to about nearly everything?
10. What is your current life motto?
11. What do people underestimate about you?
12. What do people overestimate about you?
13. What's a "perfect" day for you?
14. What do you wish you had more time for?
15. What are your expectations of a relationship?
16. What are your thoughts about online dating?
17. How has social media impacted your view of dating?
18. What are your dating pet peeves?
19. What was your best date?
20. What was your worst date?

21. What is a deal breaker in a relationship?
22. Which is more important to you: brains or looks?
23. What did you learn from a past relationship?
24. What is the best piece of advice you would give single people?
25. What do you most look forward to in the next five years?

25 Questions about Significance

1. What is significance?
2. What does significance mean to you?
3. Can significance be measured or quantified?
4. Can significance be both small and big in someone's life?
5. What is the most significant thing to you in your life right now?
6. Is being significant important to you? Why or why not?
7. Should significance be a person's goal? Why or why not?
8. What is the biggest attribute leading to significance?
9. When have you felt significant to others?
10. What makes you feel significant?
11. What are the significant relationships of your life?
12. How do you think social media impacts how people view significance?
13. How do you think faith and spirituality impact how people view significance?
14. What do you consider to be your most significant contribution to the world?
15. What type of significant contribution do you still want to make to the world?
16. What do you find your self-worth in?

17. What harms your self-worth?
18. Do you think everyone wants to be significant? Why or why not?
19. What tangible object holds significance in your life? Why?
20. What is most significant to you: helping yourself, helping your family, helping society, or helping the world?
21. Do you think someone can force themselves to be significant? Why or why not?
22. What did a past relationship teach you about significance?
23. What is your current relationship teaching you about significance?
24. Does significance equate to power? Why or why not?
25. How long does significance last?

25 Questions about
Key Moments

1. What is a treasured moment for you?
2. What is your most precious memory with someone you love?
3. What is a defining moment of your life?
4. What is your favorite moment from this summer?
5. What moment do you most remember from high school?
6. What moment do you most remember from college?
7. What holiday moment do you most remember?
8. What was an embarrassing moment in your life?
9. What was a spontaneous moment in your life?
10. What's your biggest regret in life?
11. What was the worst phase of your life?
12. What was the best phase of your life?
13. What is a moment you would want to relive?
14. What is the hardest decision you have had to make in life?
15. When is a particular time you sacrificed something?
16. What was the best date you ever went on?
17. What news event do you remember the most?
18. When is the first time you used social media?

19. What was your first cell phone?
20. When did you laugh so hard that you cried in front of another person?
21. When did you last cry in front of another person?
22. What is your favorite memory of dancing?
23. What is a moment when you knew right from wrong?
24. What moment do you most remember from the pandemic?
25. What moment led to what is now a tradition in your life or your family's life?

25 Revealing Questions about Yourself in Three Words

1. Give three words that describe your purpose in the world.
2. Give three words that describe who you are.
3. Give three words that your friends would use to describe you.
4. Give three words that describe who you were in the past.
5. Give three words that describe how the previous year was for you.
6. Give three words that describe your weaknesses.
7. Give three words that describe your work ethic.
8. Give three words that describe your career path.
9. Give three words that describe your love life.
10. Give three words that describe the most important things in your life.
11. Give three words that describe your outlook on life.
12. Give three words that describe your beliefs.
13. Give three words that describe your pet peeves.
14. Give three words that describe why you are hopeful.
15. Give three words that describe why you are excited.

16. Give three words that describe what makes you angry.
17. Give three words that describe how you deal with stress.
18. Give three words that describe your hobby.
19. Give three words that describe your obsessions.
20. Give three words that describe your job.
21. Give three words that describe your fears.
22. Give three words that describe your most important values.
23. Give three words that describe the qualities you share with your closest family member.
24. Give three words that you hope will describe you in five years.
25. Give three words that tell your life story.

CHAPTER 12

Make It
Count

Remember how I mentioned my love of fly-fishing that began in Seattle? I'm a believer in the power of mentorship, friendship, and the outdoors. In 1982, I combined my hobby and my passion when I started The Wild Adventure. Fly-fishing is at the core of my personal life and The Wild Adventure because it enriches my deepest passion—an inner walk.

The Wild Adventure is a unique fly-fishing experience that takes place throughout the summer at my ranch, the Smiling Moose. Multiple times each summer, I host a group of men at Smiling Moose for a one-week excursion. Each week, ten to twelve men from all over the country gather to float the Madison River and fish for trout in the seven private lakes on our property. They relish taking in the scenic views surrounding the ranch and spending the majority of their time fly-fishing out on the Madison River. And I lead them in open discussion about life's big questions.

But The Wild Adventure is much more than a fishing trip. For many men, it's a life-changing experience. That's because we also dedicate a lot of time to discussing some of the deeper topics of life. There's no agenda—no pledge to make or doctrines to memorize. It's just men gathering to get away from the hustle, enjoy the beauty of nature, and talk about the things that matter.

Oh, and we also have a world-class chef who feeds us extremely well. I've noticed over the years that men enjoy that kind of thing. (If The Wild Adventure sounds intriguing to you, I recommend you learn more about it at www.twa.us.)

On one final night of The Wild Adventure, there were about fifteen of us sitting around the campfire. It had been a good week. The weather had started to cool in Montana, and the night wind carried a chill. Fortunately, most of the men were bolstered by a beverage of choice. And, of course, the fire was warm.

As we gathered around the firepit, I listened while little clusters of guys drifted into the usual conversations. They talked about the fish they'd caught. They wondered what it would be like to get back to "real life" the next day. Many of them sipped their drinks in silence, just content to enjoy the company and the warmth of the fire.

I could have let things continue in that direction, and it would have been a fine evening. A perfectly mediocre conclusion to our week. But as I hope you've learned about me as you've read this little book, I'm not a fan of mediocre. And I certainly didn't feel like enduring an evening of chitchat, even if I did have a glass of my favorite wine to keep me company!

So I decided to throw out a table question. "Hey guys, let's use this time to talk about something a little out there. What would you say has been your most visceral experience with God? I'll go first."

Now, I know what you're probably thinking: you said to avoid religious questions, so what's up? The answer is that I was familiar with each of these men's stories, and we had been discussing several deep topics throughout the week, including our spiritual lives. So I felt comfortable digging a little deeper on that theme.

And the results were fascinating. Several guys shared personal encounters they had experienced with God, some of them even telling stories of when they had heard God speak to them in a powerful way. Others talked about miracles they'd experienced, and still others described moments when they had felt especially close to God because of being in a special place or going through a particularly stressful circumstance.

I was more than satisfied with the experience. What could have been just another night of banal conversations—in other words, small talk—turned into a powerful time of sharing and discovery on an intensely personal level. We all felt the depth and solemn weight of that moment.

My hope is that The Wild Adventure cultivates a space where men feel comfortable grappling with their own inner walk with complete transparency and freedom from judgment. Every year, more men become aware of the impact this trip has had on the lives of its participants, resulting in a hurried rush to sign up for the next available spot.

Wouldn't you like to experience more of those kinds of moments in your own life? I hope so, especially after you've read this book!

As we wrap up our journey together, I want to offer some final thoughts on that deeper aspect of table questions and conversations— what some may describe as the spiritual aspect. Because when you allow thoughtful people to tell their stories and share about their lives, the results can be more than interesting. They can be more than entertaining and fun.

> **Answers before questions do harm to the soul.**

They can be life-changing.

• • •

There's a quote from an author named Henri Nouwen that I really like: "Answers before questions do harm to the soul."

I think that's powerful because it's a great description of so many people, and even so many institutions, in our society. Many of us have been given the answers our whole lives. We've been told what to believe. We've been told what to do. We've been told what's right and wrong, good and bad, true and untrue.

But what we haven't done is wrestle with the deeper questions of life. The kinds of questions that start with "Why?" Think of all the people you know who have the right answer to everything—they know what they're supposed to do—and yet are still stumbling through life. Why is that? Because they haven't been shaped and pruned by the hard work of dealing with tough questions. They've just memorized the easy answers!

> **They are a way for us to go below the surface and engage in the deeper issues of life.**

As a result, their souls are harmed. Wounded. Incomplete.

One of my favorite things about table questions is that they can be a great vehicle for joining with others to explore those tough questions. The big questions. The important questions. They are a way for us to go below the surface and engage in the deeper issues of life.

Would you like to experience something like that at your dinner parties and other gatherings? There's no formula to experiencing life-changing moments, but I do have a few tips to offer.

First and foremost, understand that you can't force those deeper moments—those spiritual encounters. They have to come about organically. Don't think, *I'm going to have my best friends over, and I'm going to change their lives.* It won't happen like that.

The second thing I would say is that you should never be afraid to ask bigger questions. Don't be afraid to ask the kinds of questions that point to those deeper, more transcendent topics and ideas. Because although it's true that you can't force people to have significant encounters and life-changing moments, you can be certain they won't experience anything big or meaningful if you never give them the chance!

> **Don't be afraid to ask the kinds of questions that point to those deeper, more transcendent topics and ideas.**

Think of this question as an example: "What do you think is behind the world, the universe, and everything we see?" That's a good question, but you're likely to get a lot of standard answers in response. People will repeat what they learned in their catechisms or their Sunday school classes, or whatever their parents told them when they got old enough to ask who made the sun and the sky.

But what if you encourage people to go deeper? What if, after everyone spends a few minutes giving those standard answers, you respond by asking, "Why do you believe what you just said?"

That's helping people wrestle with the questions. That's giving your guests an opportunity to engage with an important topic in a way they may not have tried before. And that means you've created an opportunity for truly meaningful conversation.

Finally, let's explore what you should do if someone experiences something significant, even potentially life-changing, during one of your gatherings. Because it really does happen. I've seen it dozens of times—maybe hundreds.

I've seen large, rough-talking men break down in tears after sharing about a wound they received from their father when they were a child. I've seen people share deep and moving soliloquies about their spouses that made everyone else cry. And I've seen guests confess their struggles with addiction or abuse or depression or any number of afflictions.

So, how should you respond as the host in those moments?

In my experience, the worst thing you can do is pretend nothing happened. Some people think that's a good idea because they don't want to put their guest on the spot, or maybe because they're embarrassed about what they just witnessed. But ignoring a significant revelation in someone's life can be hurtful at best and create lasting scars at worst.

When someone has become emotional or overwhelmed after sharing something personal, the appropriate response is to hit the emergency button. Stop the presses. Take a break from the usual routine.

I like to speak directly to that person and acknowledge what happened. "Wow, Fred, that was really heavy. You must be experiencing a lot of emotions right now." Or, "Jane, that seemed to be a real breakthrough for you. Am I right?" Or, "Hey, Tom, I want to say that I'm proud of you for being so open and honest just now. I really appreciate what you shared, and I think everyone here feels the same way."

> If something significant happens during a table conversation, make sure to acknowledge it. Make sure to give that moment the respect and the weight it deserves.

Next, it's often helpful to allow your other guests to both participate in the moment and offer help or encouragement. You might say, "I think that was a powerful moment, Steve. Does anyone else feel the same way?" Or, "Who else has experienced something similar to what Jim just described?" Or even, "Who would like to pray for Betsy right now?"

The point is, if something significant happens during a table conversation, make sure to acknowledge it. Make sure to give that moment the respect and the weight it deserves. Trust me, you won't regret it—and neither will your guests!

• • •

As we bring this book to a close, remember that you never again have to settle for small talk. With table questions, you can find a world of wonderful gatherings and meaningful conversations. All you need is to plan ahead, ask the right questions, stay in control of the conversation, and keep things fun.

Trust me, if I can do it—and I've been asking table questions in one form or fashion for almost forty years now—you can do it too!

Think about it: you have the opportunity right now to make your gatherings and get-togethers more than just a polite exchange of chitchat and transactional conversations. You can make them significant, fascinating, and fun!

That's the power of table questions—of turning small talk into Big Talk. And the more you tap into that power, the more you'll find that table questions really are the most delicious part of a meal!

As I share this concept with people at our dinner parties and The Wild Adventure and now with you through this book, here is what I imagine and dream of: I believe that we all can become conveners. I believe that what may be the only dinner each week that you have with your family could be one that is meaningful and intentional. At tables in cities across the country, people are saying, "I was at a dinner party or around this campfire or I was reading a book, and this guy asked a question at the table, and I thought that might be fun for us to do."

I imagine that people gathering around tables of all sizes, at all times of day and serving all types of food are being asked questions like: What's been the most important issue on your mind this past year? What's had the biggest impact on your life? What are you the most excited about in the next thirty days? And many, many other questions—and then time spent listening to each other.

By saying that and suggesting it to others at your table, it makes that first step much easier for someone else, then someone else, then someone else. You're helping them to do that. You're passing the conductor baton on and on and on. The implications could be far-reaching.

So here's to all of you, my fellow conveners.

For videos and more helpful
information on how to turn small talk
into big talk, please visit
www.TurningSmallTalkIntoBigTalk.com

Acknowledgements

It's easy to cultivate ideas, but the challenge is to be proactive in following through. Whether it's starting a new venture or writing a book, I understand the dedication required to bring it to completion. I could not do it without people in my life to support me.

I am thankful for the people in my life who encouraged me to write this book. I follow the life philosophy "Take the first step." It has guided me in my early days as a novice entrepreneur, and over forty years later, it is with that same mentality that I approach every professional and personal decision. I could not do this without the support of my wife, Carol, whose visionary mindset and partnership continues to inspire me today. I also can't miss giving Champ another callout, for all the joy he has brought us.

I also have to pay homage to authors whose books have guided me through life. The directions and lessons I learned in reading *Wild at Heart,* by John

Eldredge, and *The Road Less Traveled,* by M. Scott Peck, are ones I continue to draw from, and if what I have written in this book has had even a sliver of their impact, it would make me so happy.

Organizations such as Young Life have been pivotal in my life, from the experiences I had guiding teens to introducing me to important people, such as Carol, and hobbies I love, such as fly-fishing.

About the Author

Jan Janura is a serial entrepreneur, out-of-the-box innovator, and, according to Gallup's StrengthsFinder test, a futurologist. His insight has helped him establish prosperous businesses across a diverse range of markets. His first job was with YOUNG LIFE as an area director in Seattle, which was a position that he loved, but he kept hearing a call to enter the business world. Jan saw his career take off in 1977 after making a call to his friend, and now wife, Carol Anderson, who he had met while he was getting his masters degree. He and Carol were both volunteer leaders at a YOUNG LIFE club in Burbank, California, from 1971 to 1973. Carol had just left her eight-year position as fashion designer and had plans to renounce her job in design but wanted to stay in the industry. She immediately received several offers from other companies, but Jan convinced her that they should start a company together! Jan felt a calling to pioneer a new business venture, and together they forged a partnership.

With Carol's vision for fashion and Jan's business insight, Carol Anderson INC. was born in a garage in Burbank, California. Four months later, they received their first order from Nordstrom. Twenty-five years later, disturbing changes were taking place in retailing through mass consolidation. Jan saw this and realized that they had to change their distribution model. One morning at breakfast on the proverbial napkin where great ideas are born it hit him — let's sell Carol's great fashion at house parties! In 2003 his idea became CAbi—for Carol Anderson by invitation—with ten sales consultants. By 2012, nine and a half years later, there were over 3,200 CAbi consultants and the company was selling several hundred million annually!

In 1976, Jan combined hobby and passion when he started The Wild Adventure. Multiple times each summer, Jan hosts a group of men at his Smiling Moose Ranch in Montana for a one-week excursion. He leads them in open discussions about life's big questions, and they relish the scenic views surrounding his ranch and spend their free time fly-fishing on the Madison River.

CAbi and The Wild Adventure are two of Jan Janura's most notable accomplishments to date. He credits their success to his nurturing nature and believes every entrepreneur is capable of the same triumph if they pursue their passions and follow their calling. To quote Proverbs 24:3, "Any enterprise is built by wise planning, becomes strong through common sense, and profits wonderfully by keeping abreast of the facts."

Jan is a firm believer that once you feel an urge to cultivate an idea, you should be proactive in this pursuit. This energy, he believes, sets an entrepreneur apart from ninety percent of people. While fervor is what should drive an entrepreneur's goals, Jan Janura has meticulously built his endeavors with bridled passion. Today, Jan is pioneering his next big idea and truly forging new paths for anyone who connects with him.

When he is not busy developing a new business venture, Jan is occupied with his hobbies. You can find him in his backyard fly fishing on the Madison River, on the golf course, or reading a book.

Notes

1 Norman Maclean, *A River Runs through It and Other Stories,
   Twenty-Fifth Anniversary Edition*, (Chicago: University Of Chicago
   Press, 2001).

2 Herbert Hoover, *Fishing for Fun: And to Wash Your Soul,* (New York:
   Random House, 1963)

3 Dale Carnegie, Dorothy Carnegie, and Arthur R Pell, *How to Win
   Friends & Influence People*, (New York: Gallery Books, 1998).

4 Sims Wyeth, "10 Ways Great Speakers Capture People's Attention."
   Inc.com. March 5, 2014, https://www.inc.com/sims-wyeth/how-to-
   capture-and-hold-audience-attention.html.

5 Jack Schafer and Marvin Karlins, *The Like Switch : An Ex-FBI Agent's
   Guide to Influencing, Attracting, and Winning People Over*, (New York:
   Atria Paperback, An Imprint Of Simon & Schuster Inc., 2019).

6 Robert N. Bostrom and Nancy Grant Harrington, "An Exploratory
   Investigation of Characteristics of Compulsive Talkers,"
   Communication Education 48 (1, 1999): 73–80, https://doi.
   org/10.1080/03634529909379154.

7 Lindsey Holmes, "10 Thoughts Introverts Have about Parties,"
   Huffpost, October 28, 2015, https://www.huffpost.com/entry/
   introverts-and-parties_n_562e9982e4b0631799of1037.

8 Sarah E. Davies, "Socializing as an Introvert," Well, Well, Well: A
   UVA Law Student Affairs Blog, February 5, 2020. https://www.law.
   virginia.edu/wellness/socializing-introvert-0.

9 Rico Gagliano and Brendan Francis Newnam, "10 Tips for

Fascinating Table Talk at Your next Dinner Party," *The New York Times*, November 2, 2017, https://www.nytimes.com/2017/11/02/magazine/10-tips-for-fascinating-table-talk-at-your-next-dinner-party.html.

Celeste Anne Headlee, *We Need to Talk: How to Have Conversations That Matter.* (New York: Harper Wave, 2018).

Elizabeth Sarah Larkin, "20 Unacceptable Things People Do at Dinner Parties," TheRecipe, November 13, 2018, https://www.therecipe.com/unacceptable-things-people-do-dinner-parties/.

Marley Duchovnay, Casey Moore, and Gina M. Masullo, "How to Talk to People Who Disagree with You Politically," Center for Media Engagement, July 2020, https://mediaengagement.org/ research/divided-communities.

Sarah Todd, "The Best Conversation Topics for Dinner Parties, according to Experts," Quartz, May 15, 2018, https://qz.com/quartzy/1277057/the-best-conversation-topics-for-dinner-parties-according-to-experts/.

Clemency Burton-Hill, "What Does a Conductor Actually Do?" BBC, October 31, 2014, https://www.bbc.com/culture/article/20141029-what-do-conductors-actually-do.

Mark Wigglesworth, "Music Is an Act of Communication. Without Anyone Listening It Doesn't Exist," *The Guardian*, September 29, 2020, https://www.theguardian.com/music/2020/sep/29/conductor-mark-wigglesworth-comment-classical-music.

Jennifer Tung and Lisa Milbr, "10 Tips for Making Small Talk Less Awkward," Real Simple, September 24, 2021, https://www.realsimple.com/work-life/work-life-etiquette/manners/10-big-rules-small-talk.

Jennifer Russell, "How to Be Interesting at a Dinner Party." The Splendid Table, June 28, 2013, https://www.splendidtable.org/story/2013/06/28/how-to-be-interesting-at-a-dinner-party.

Ximena Vengoechea, *Listen like You Mean It: Reclaiming the Lost Art of True Connection*, (New York: Portfolio, 2021).

Ximena Vengoechea, "Why It's So Important to Stay Present in Our Conversations," Thriveglobal.com, March 30, 2021, https://

thriveglobal.com/stories/the-importance-of-staying-pres-
ent-in-our-conversations/.

20 Karie Tennant, Ashley Long, and Tammy J. Toney-Butler, "Active
Listening," National Library of Medicine, May 8, 2022, https://www.
ncbi.nlm.nih.gov/books/NBK442015/.

21 Carol Kinsey Goman, *The Silent Language of Leaders: How Body
Language Can Help or Hurt How You Lead,* (San Francisco: Jossey-Bass,
2011).

22 Carol Kinsey Goman, "10 Body Language Myths That Limit
Success," Carol Kensey Goman, carolkenseygoman.com, https://
carolkinseygoman.com/10-body-language-myths-that-limit-
success.